How putrid is the matter which underlies everything. Water, dust, bones, stench.
Fine marbles are the calluses of the earth and gold and silver its sediments
and our garments of matted hairs, with dye of purple blood from shellfish.
Even our breath is another thing and will change from this to that.

Soon very soon you will be ashes or a skeleton, and simply a name
or not even that.

Marcus Aurelius

Death *and* Other Belongings

Will Green

GOST

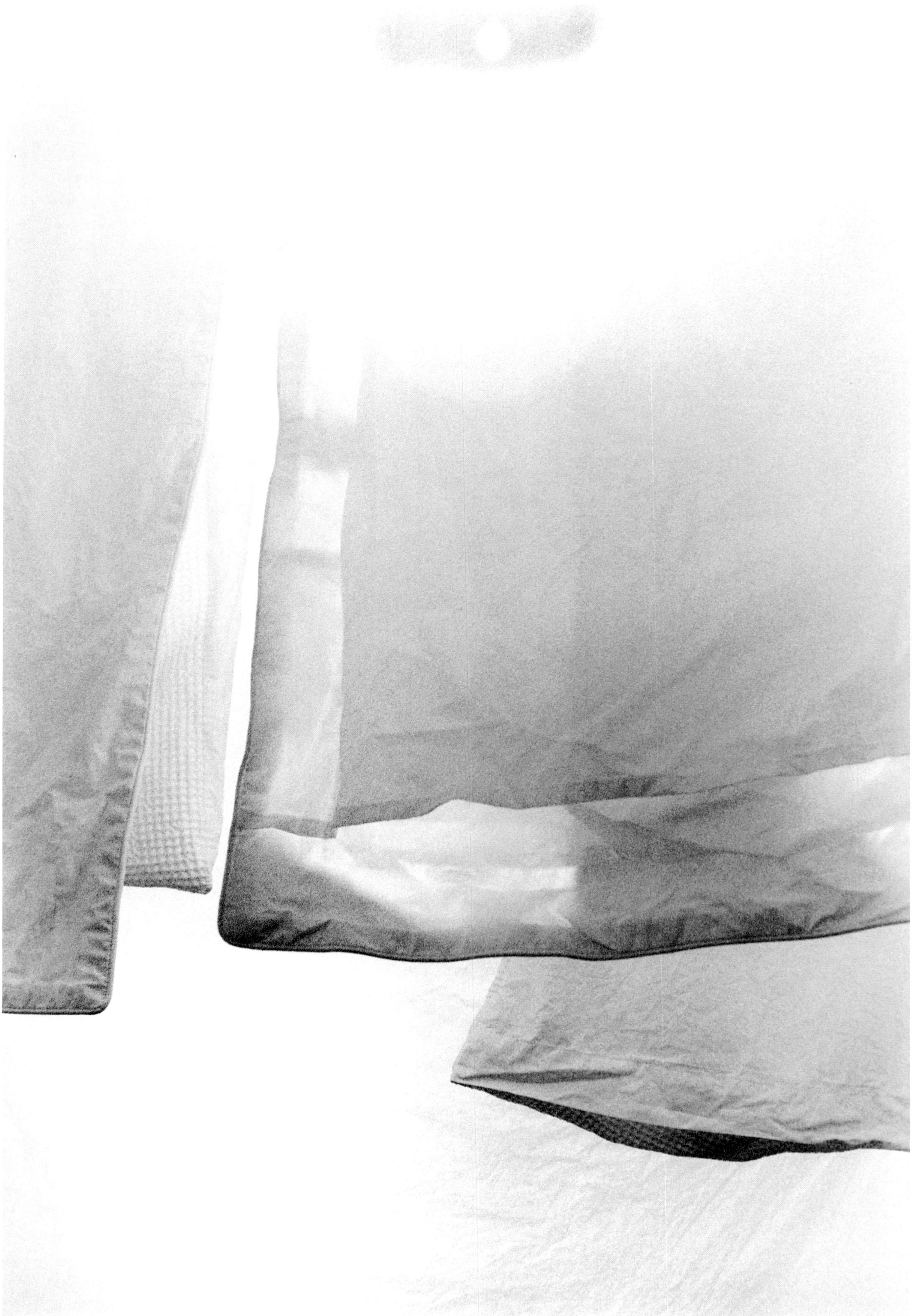

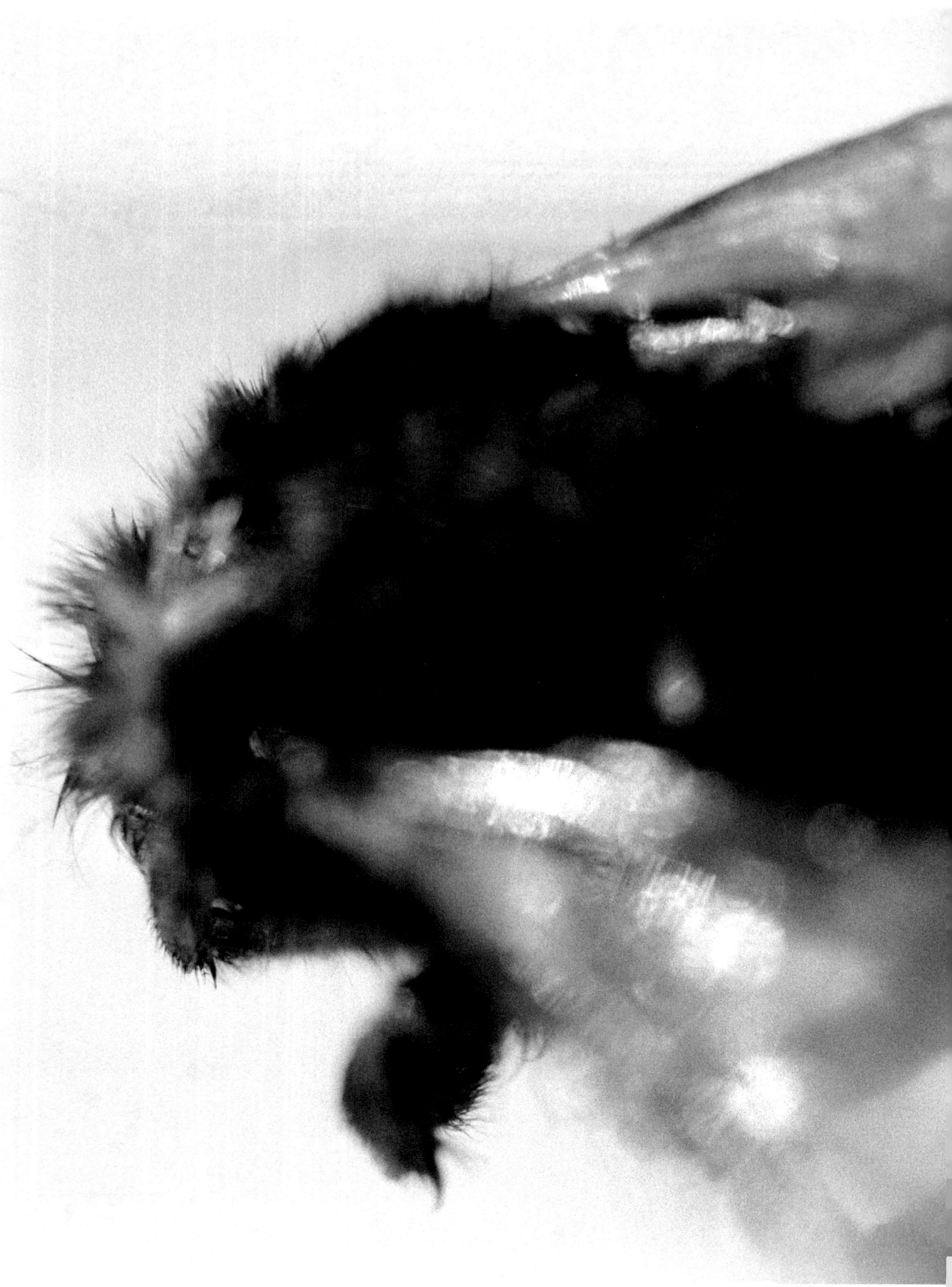

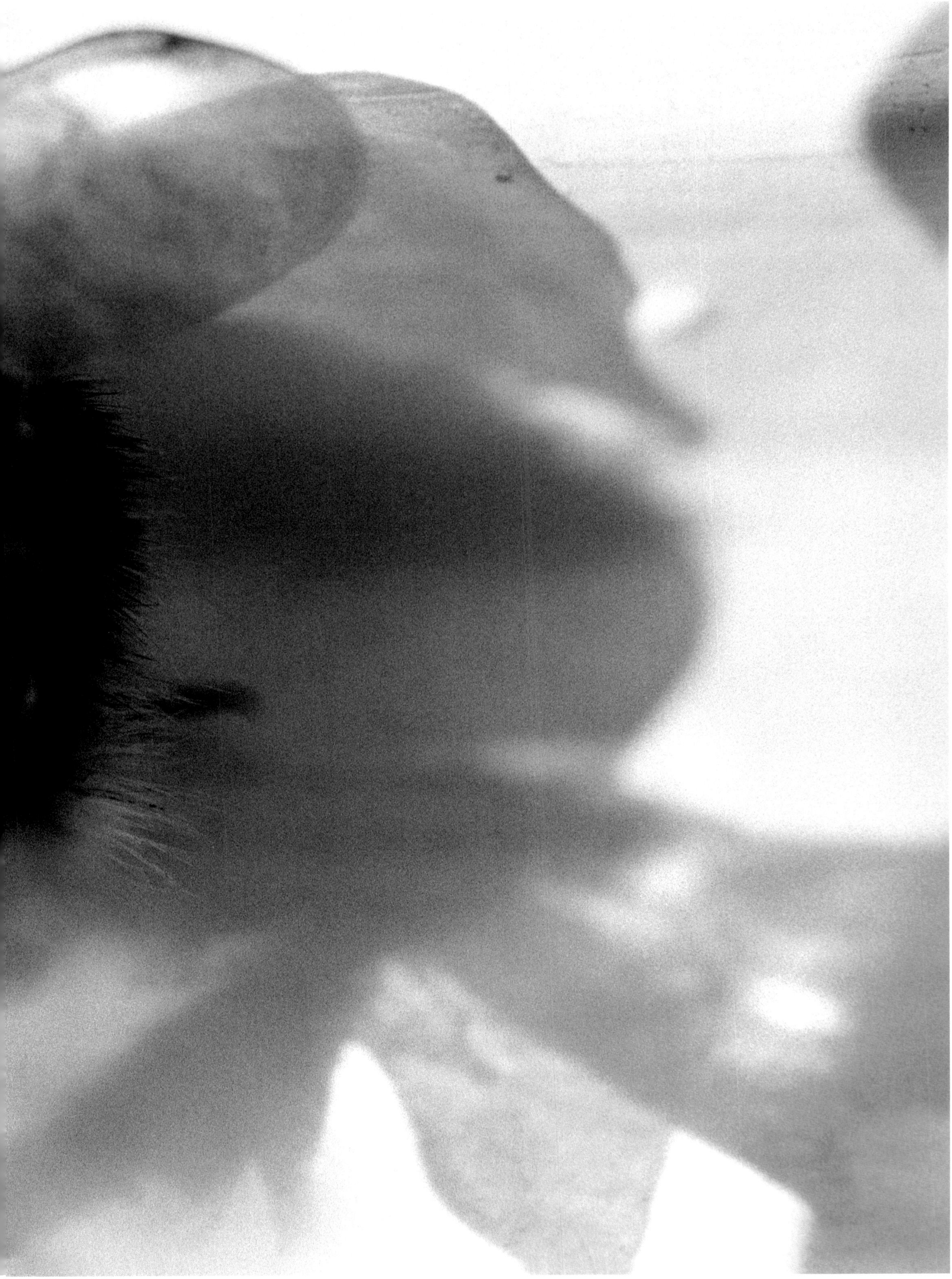

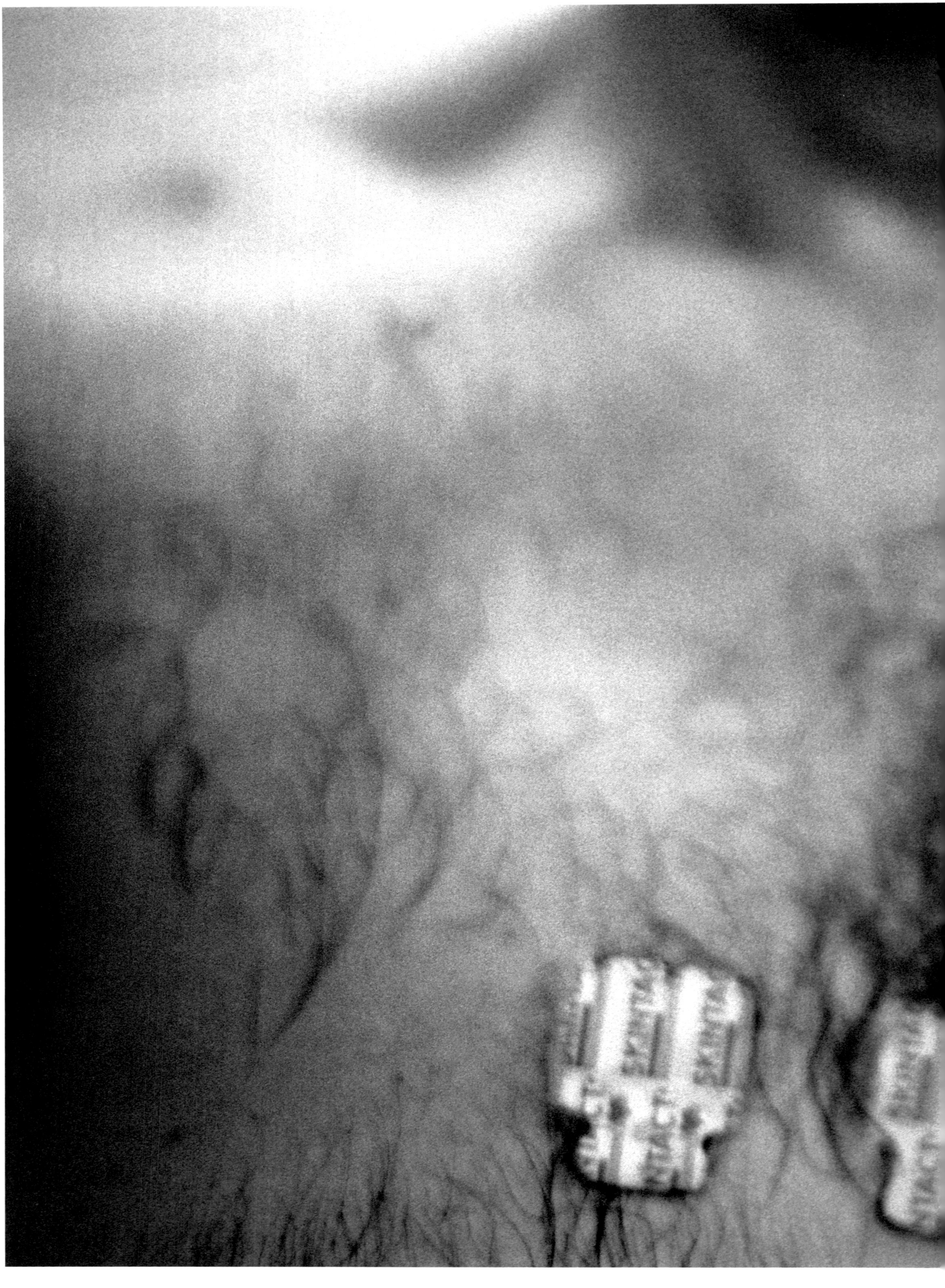

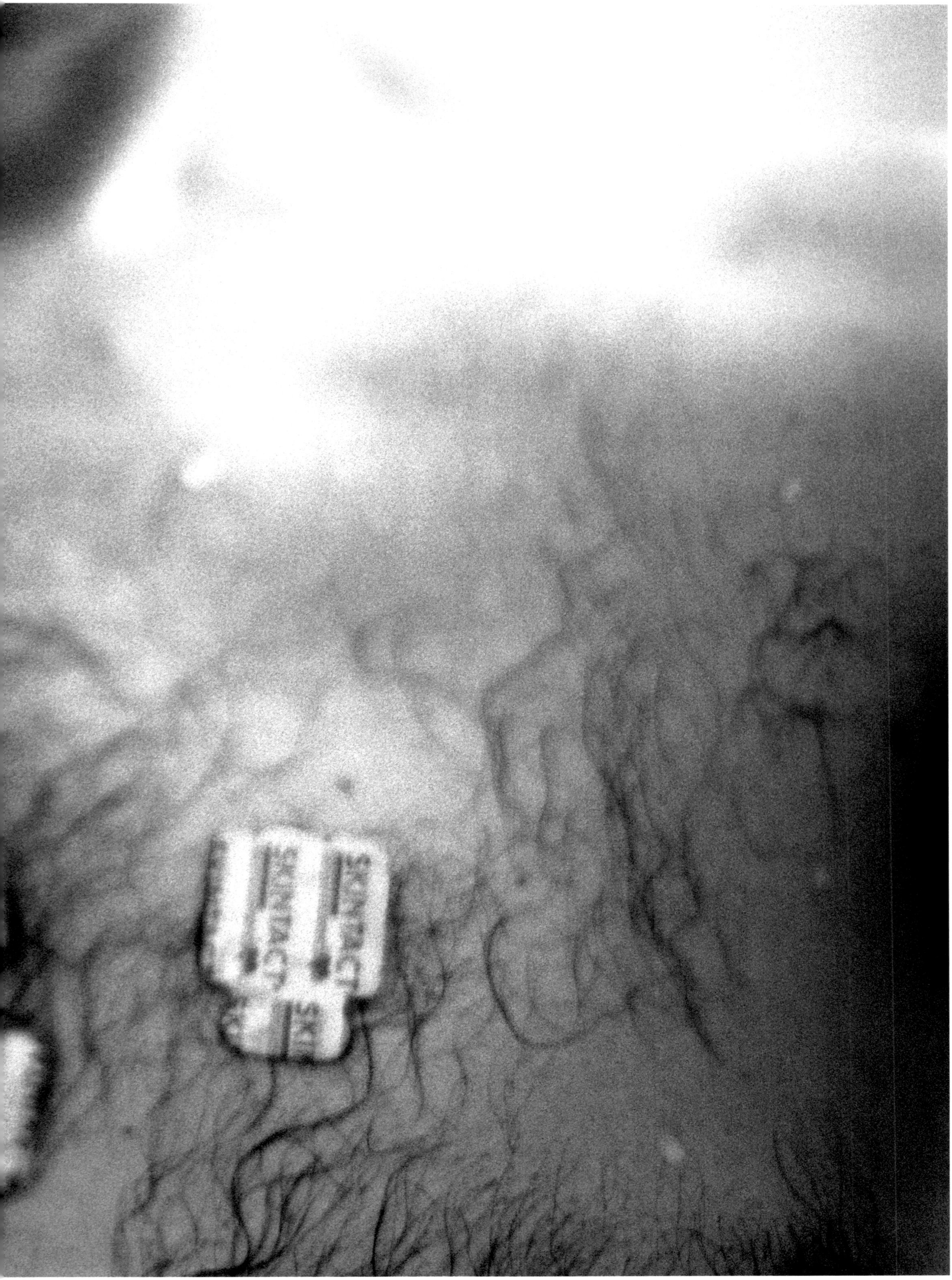
SKINTACT

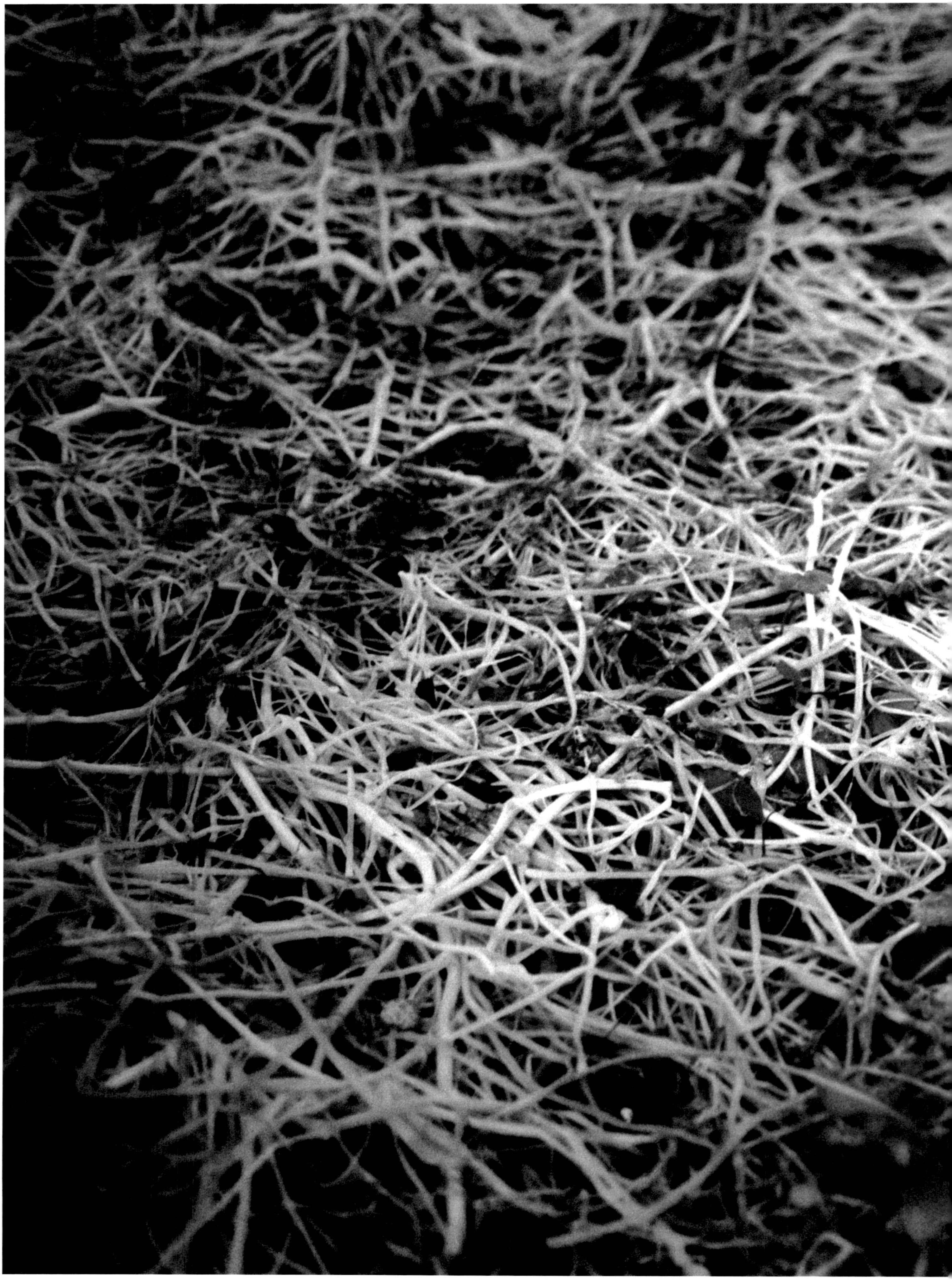

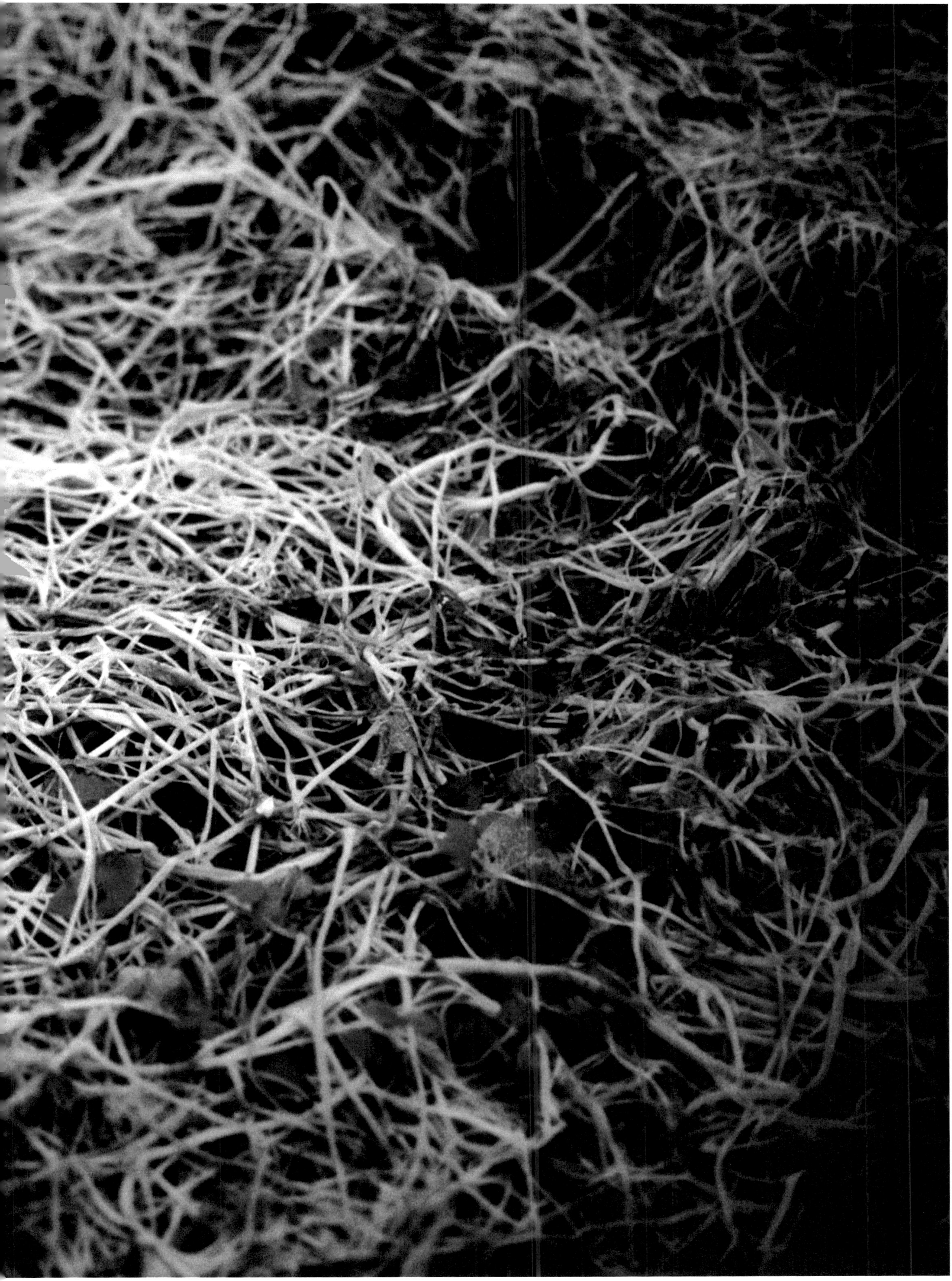

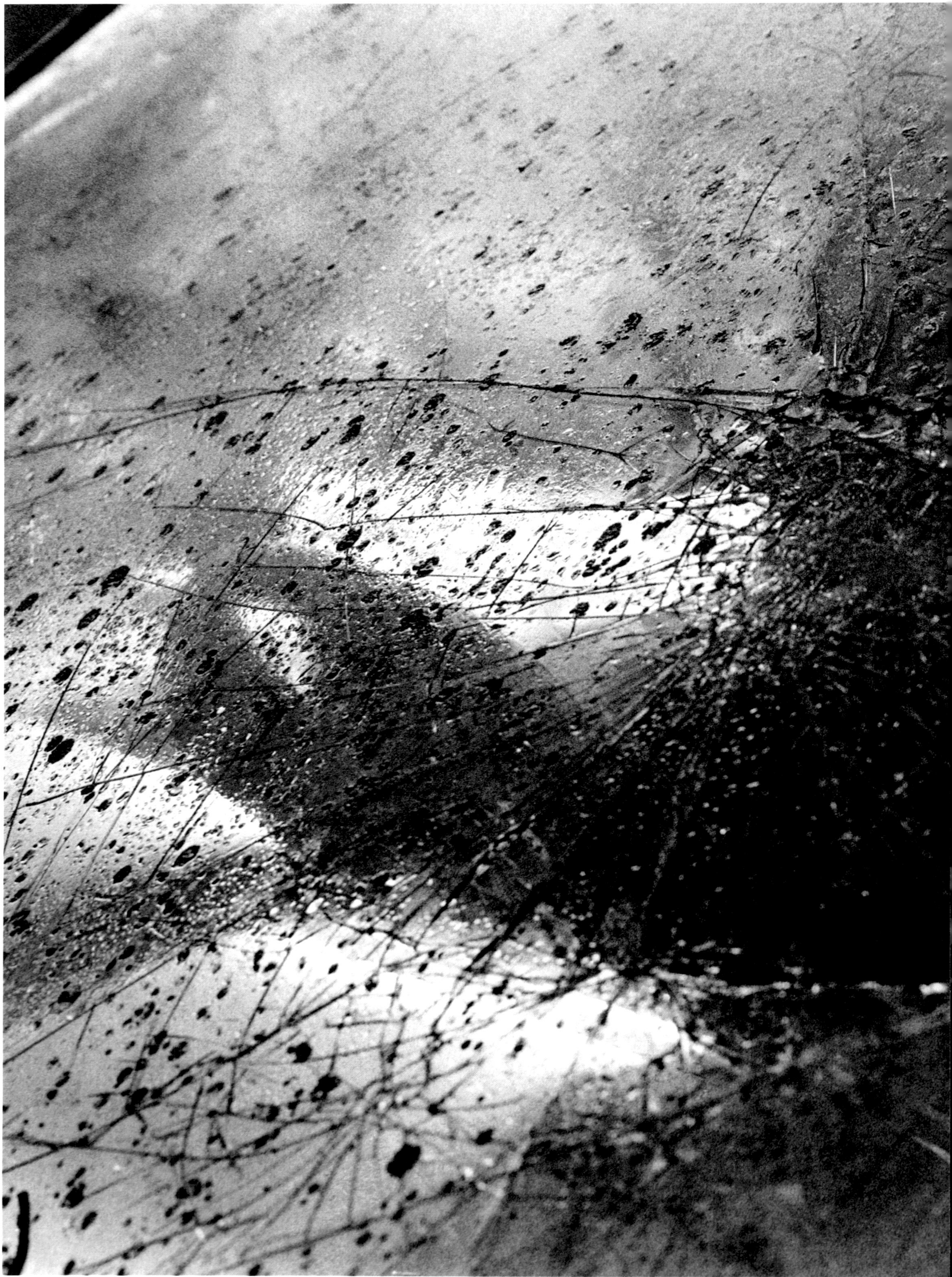

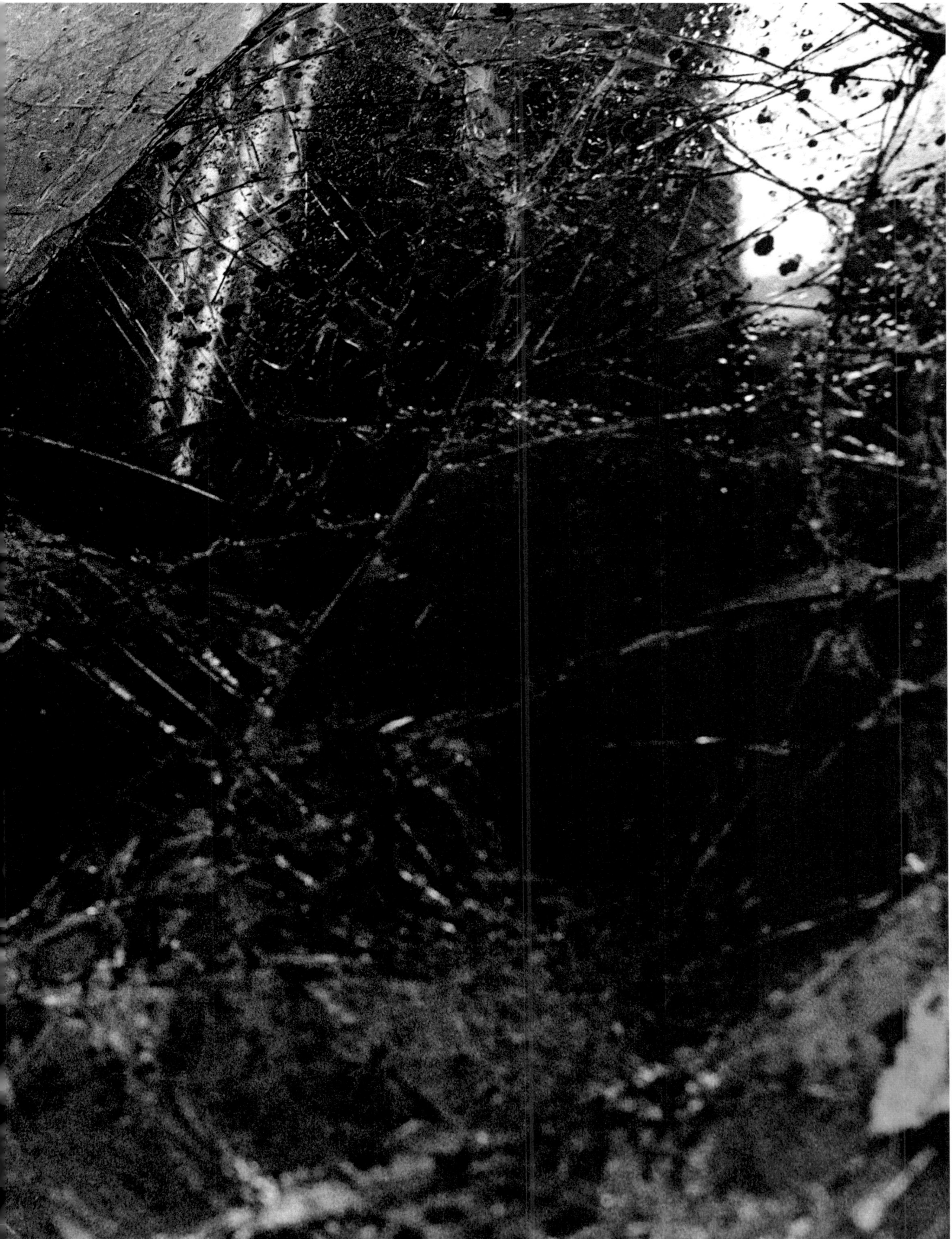

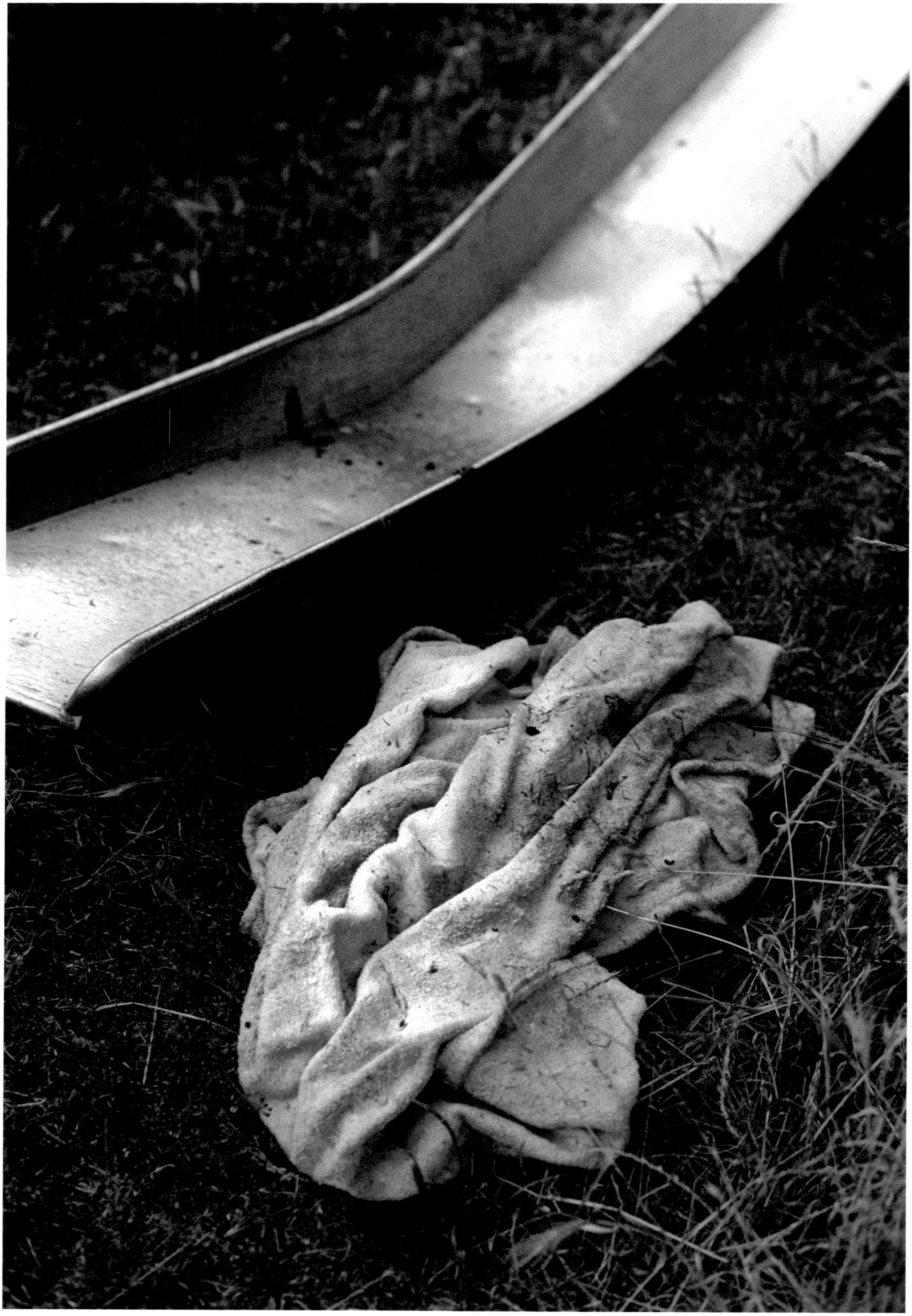

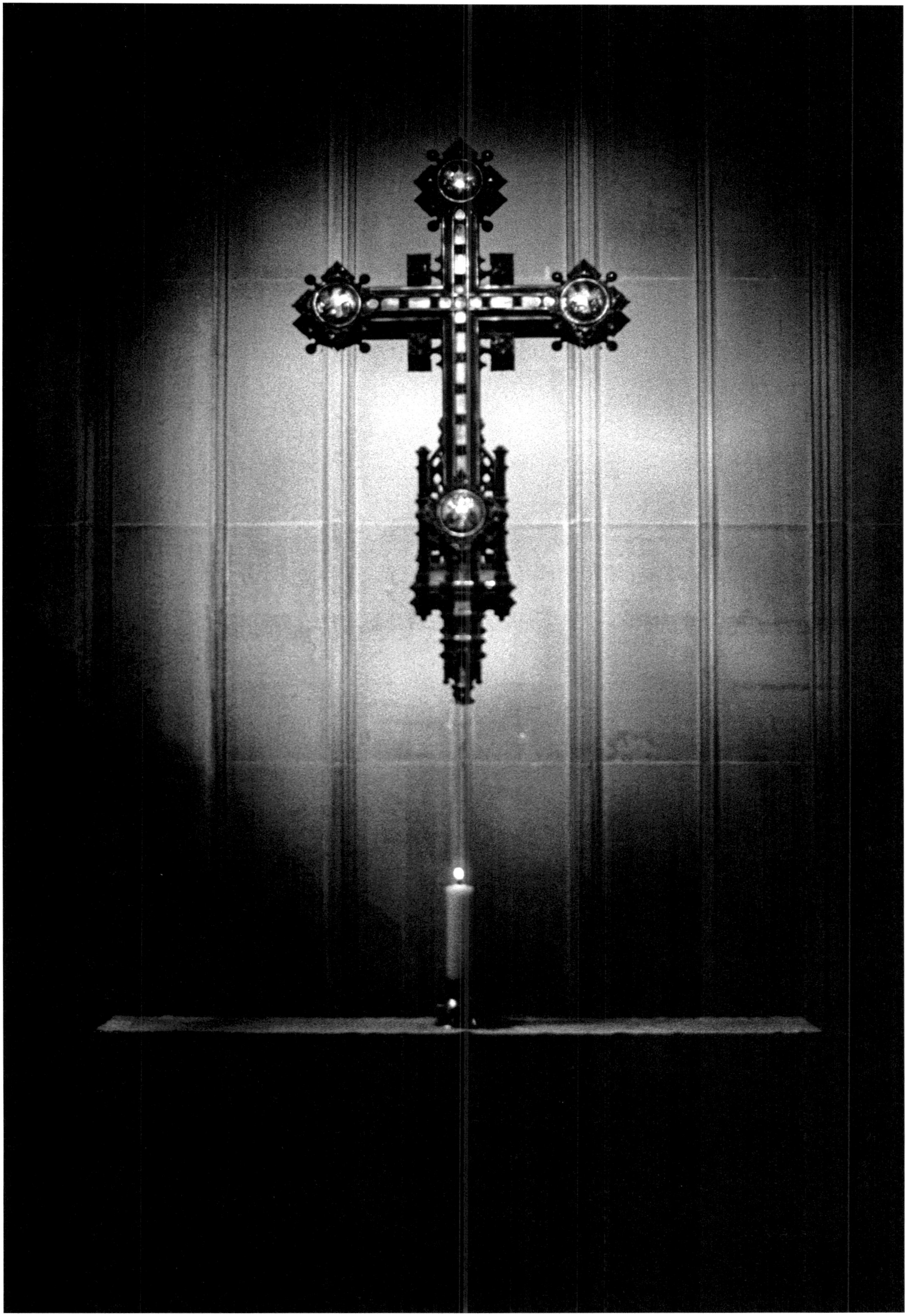

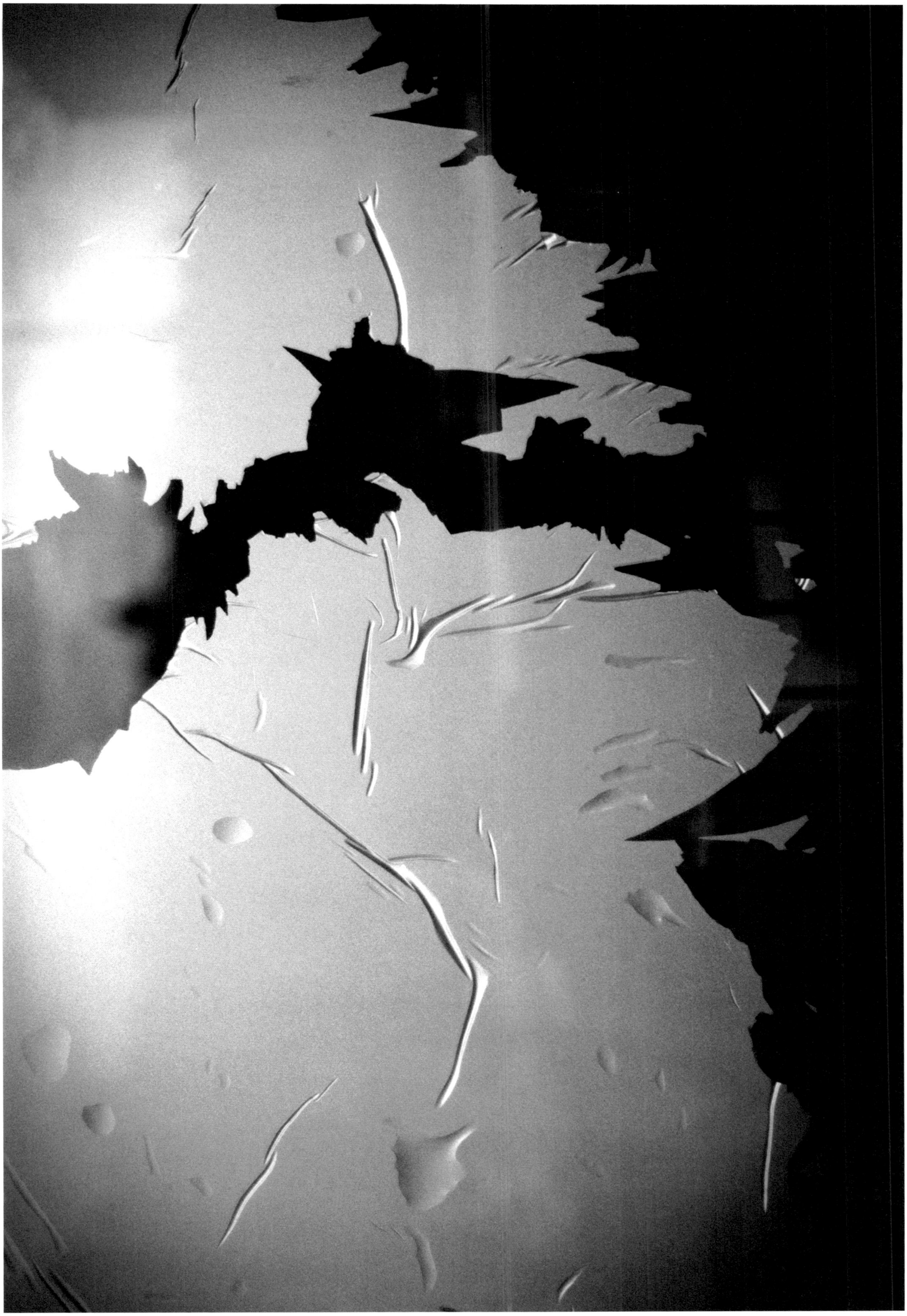

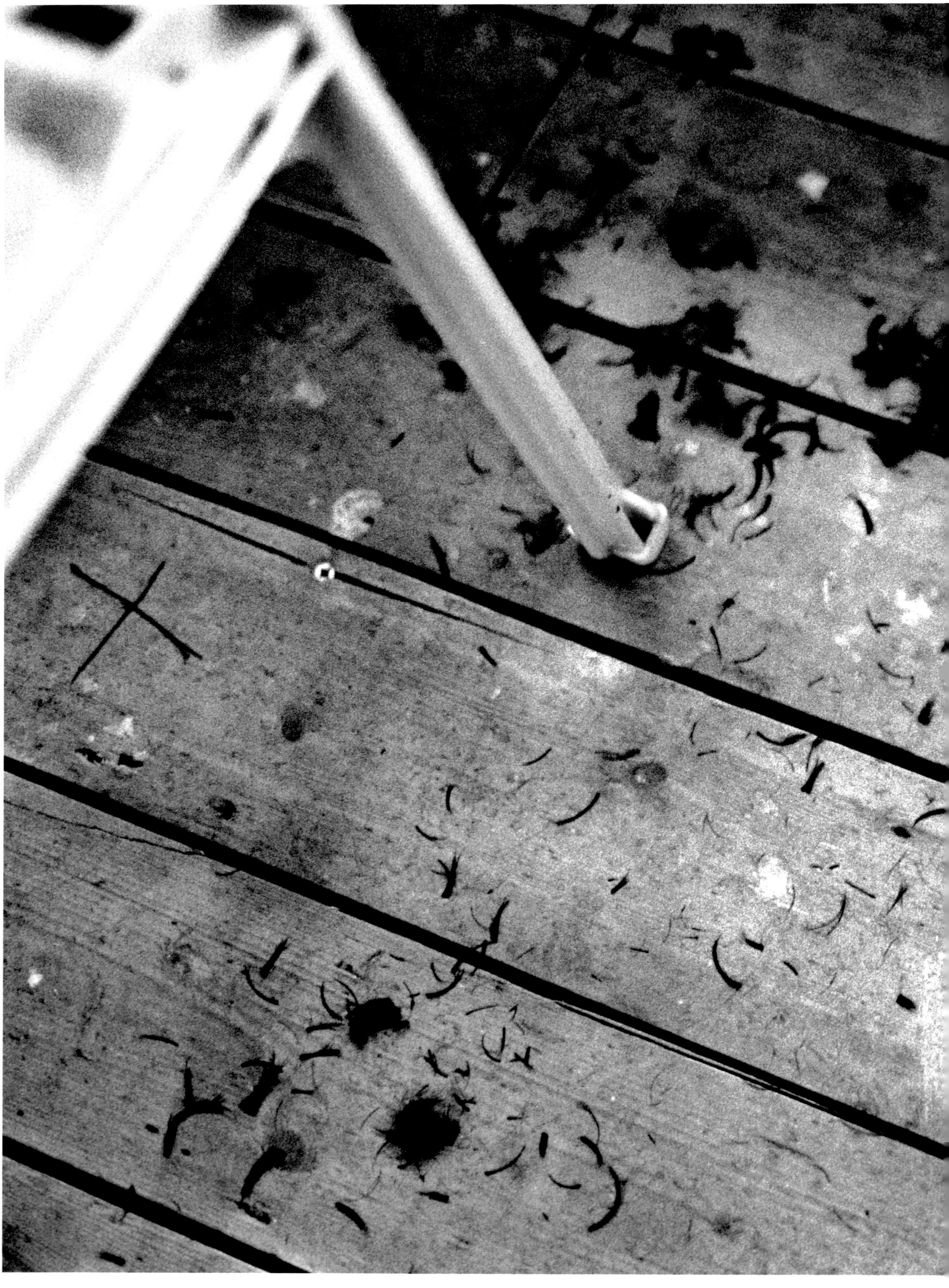

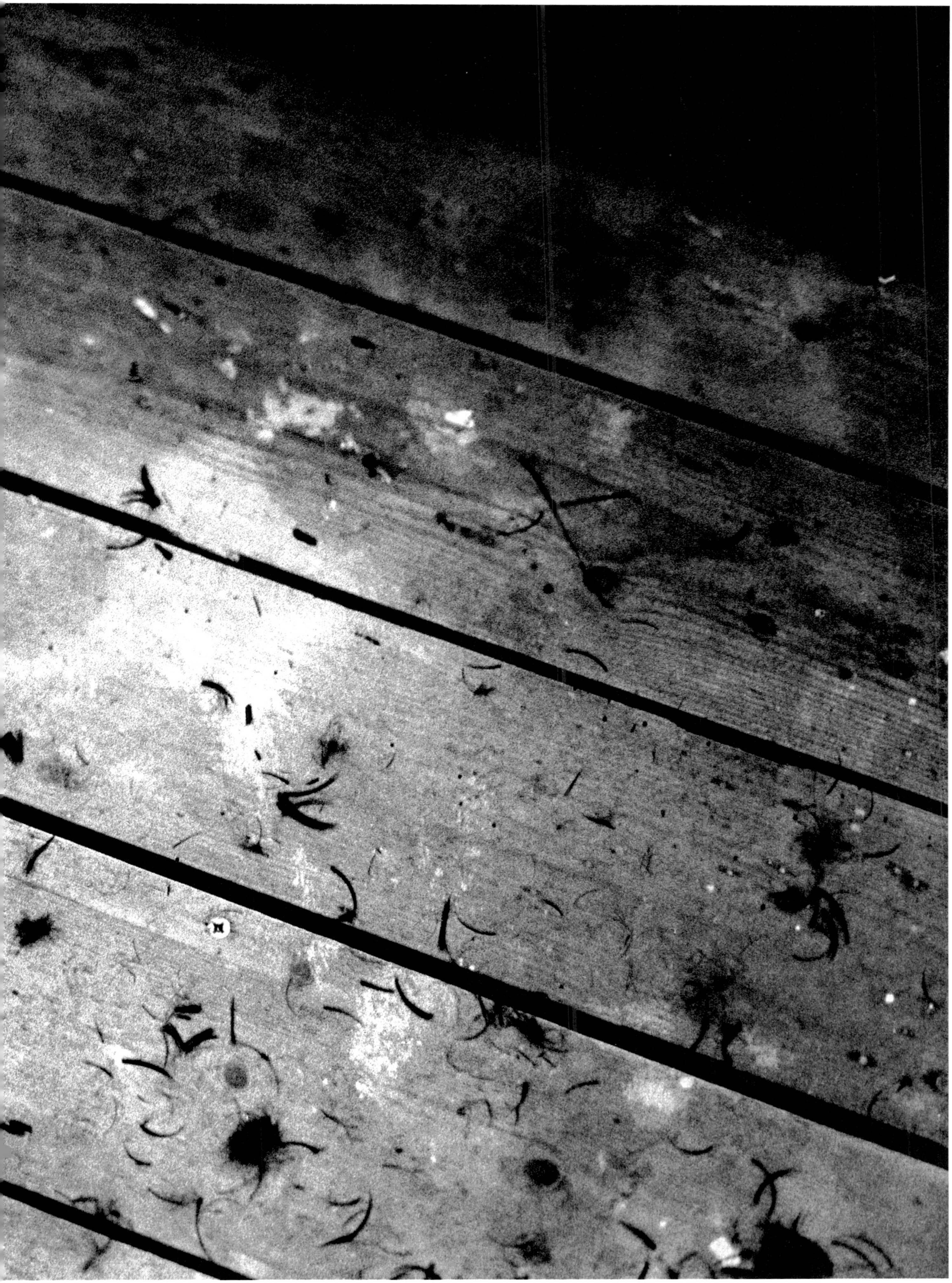

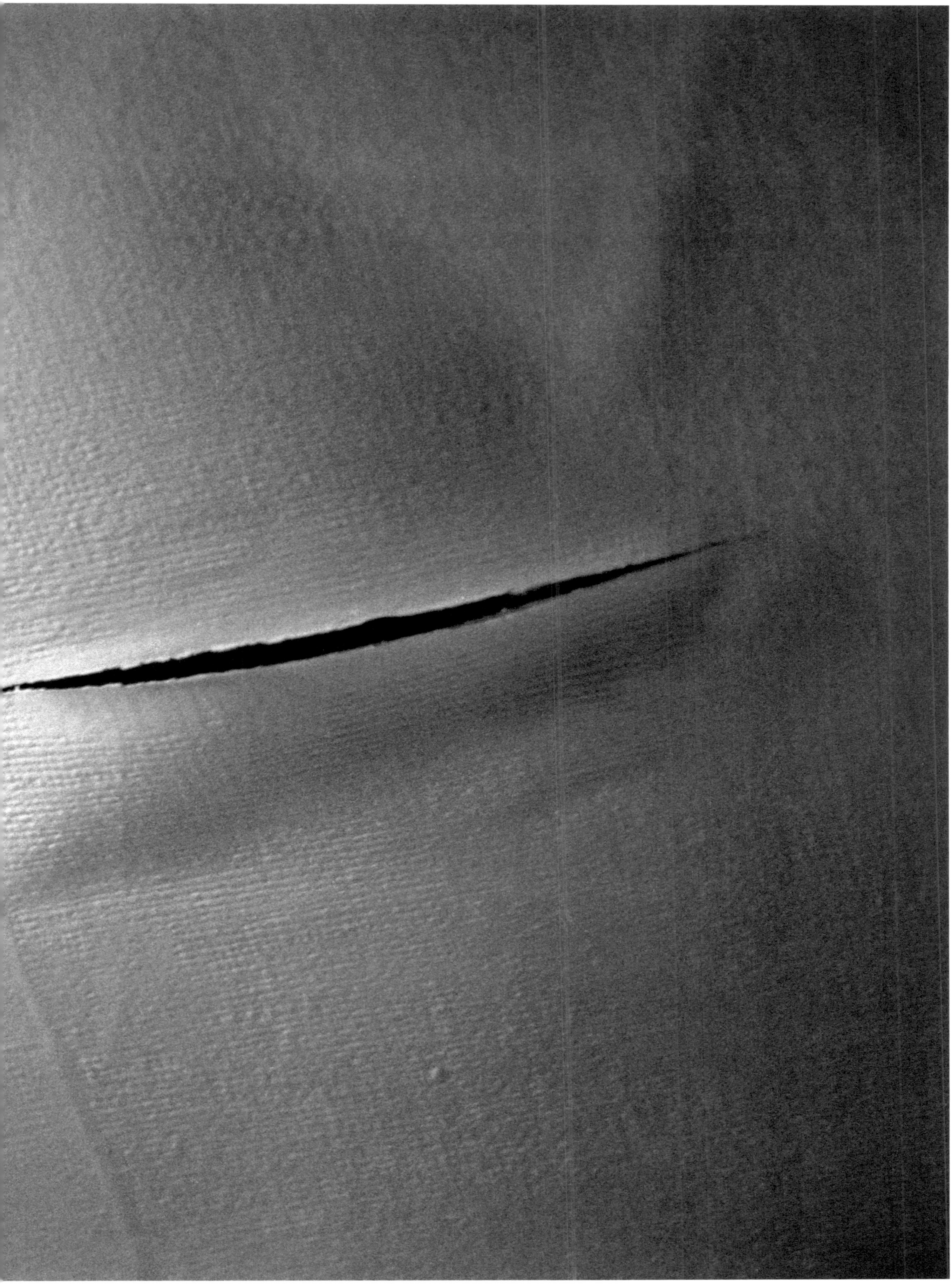

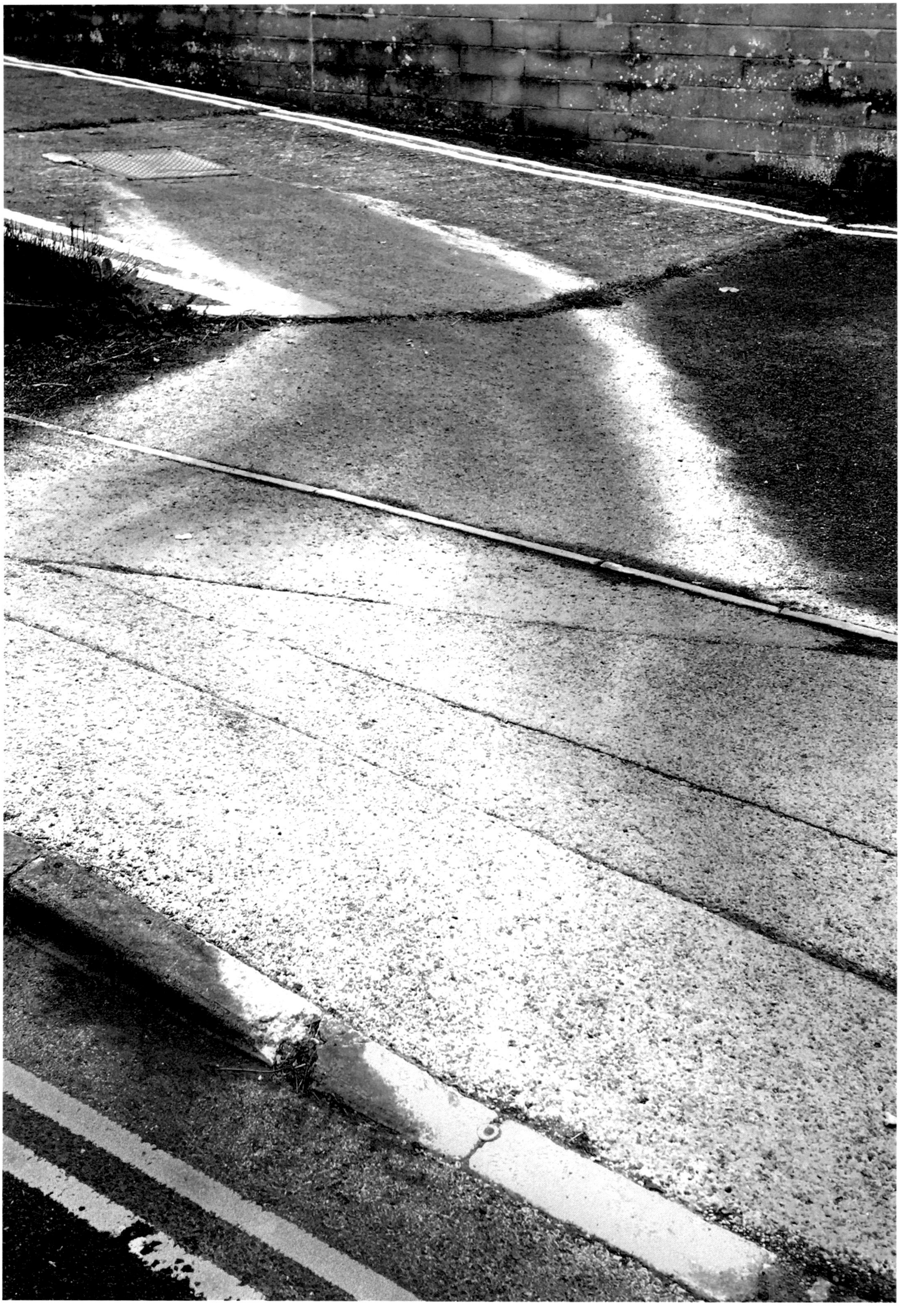

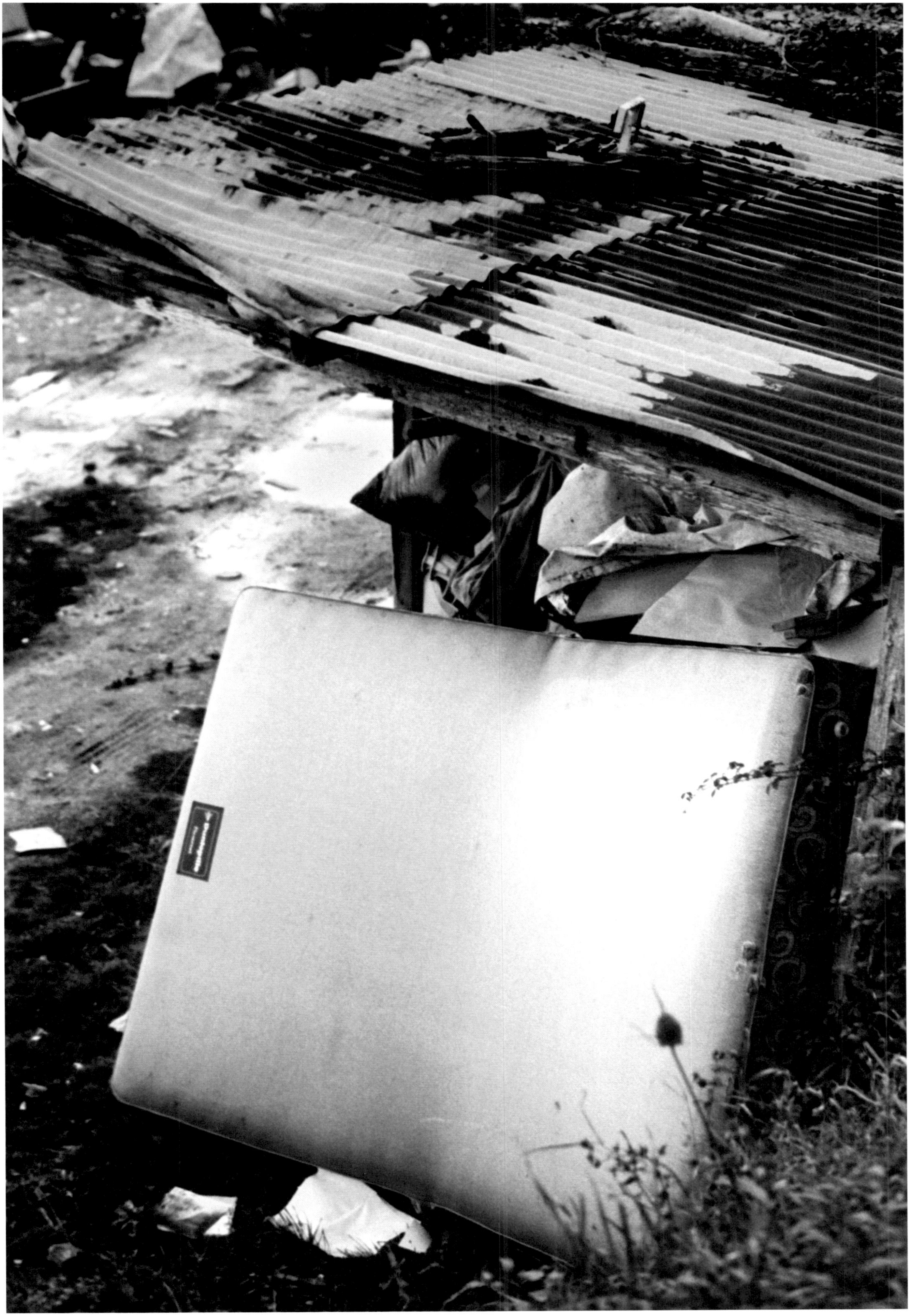

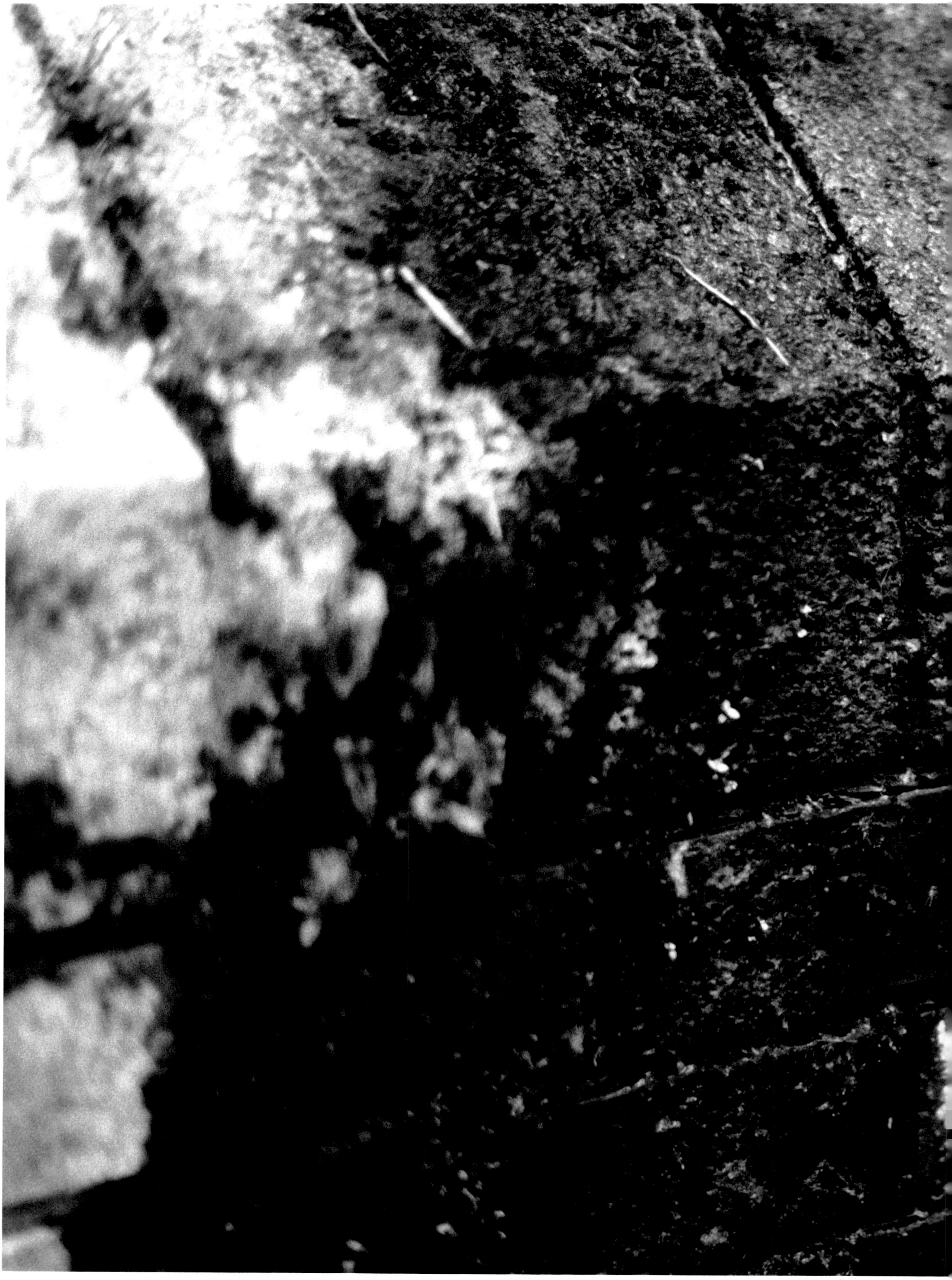

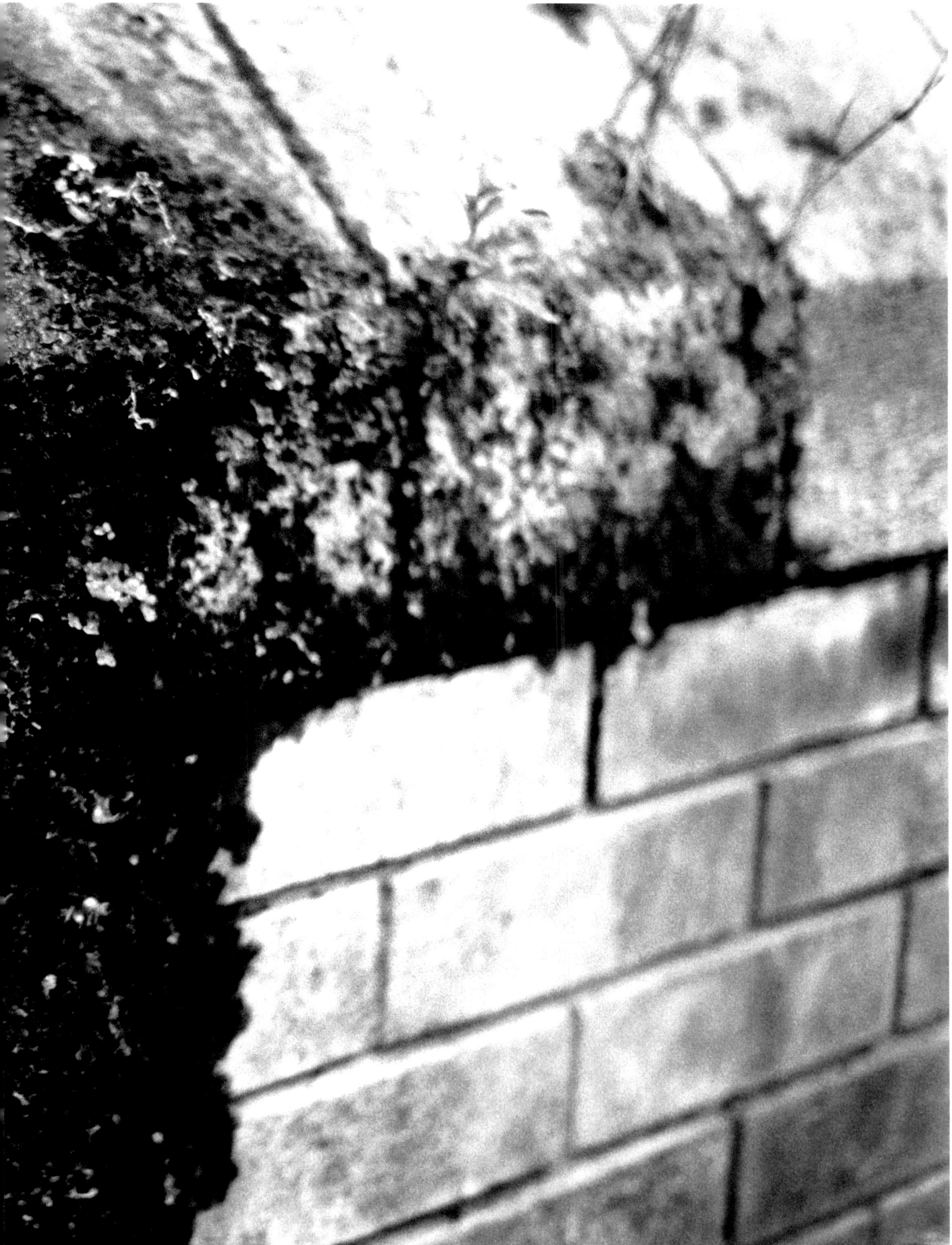

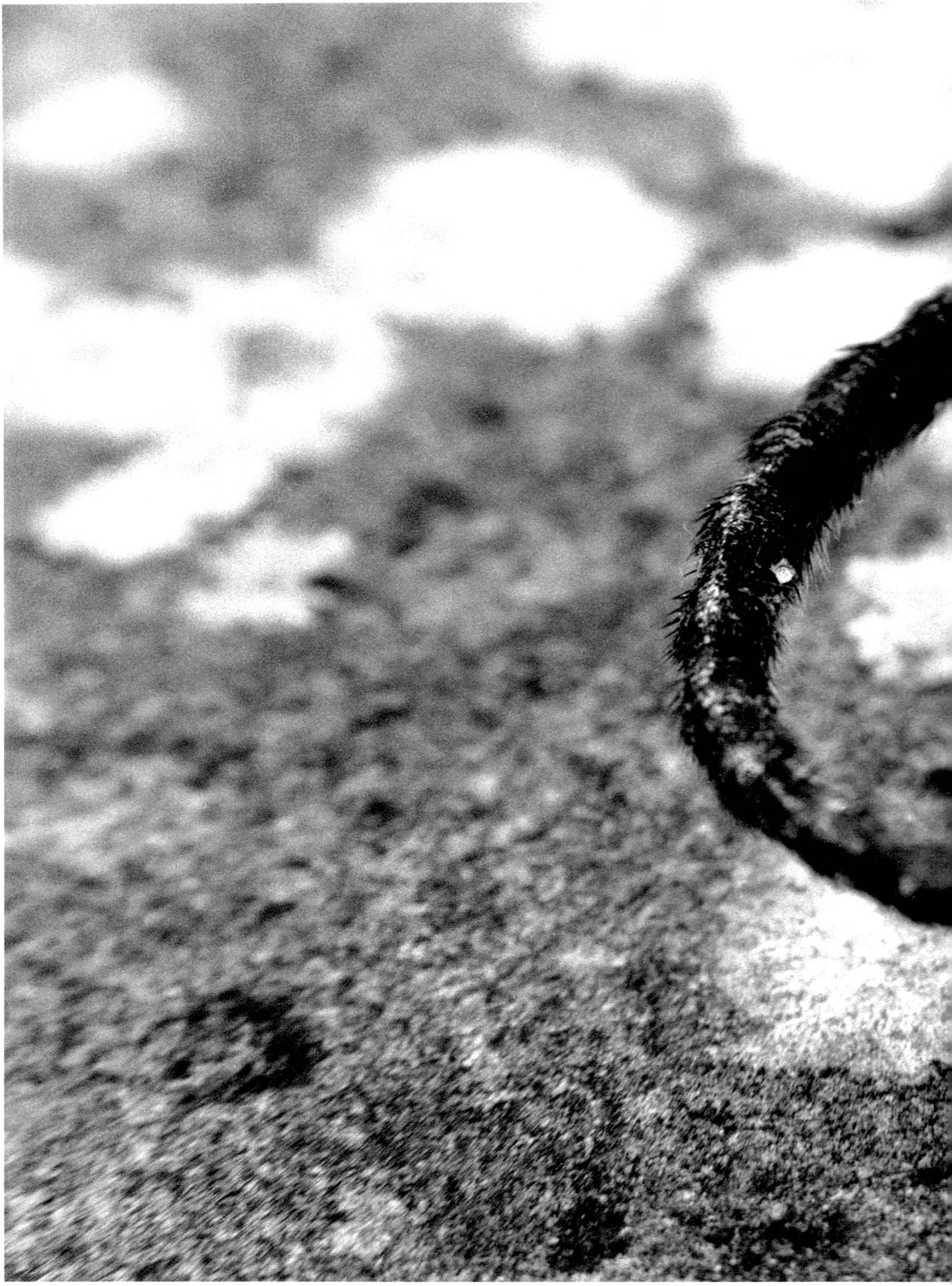

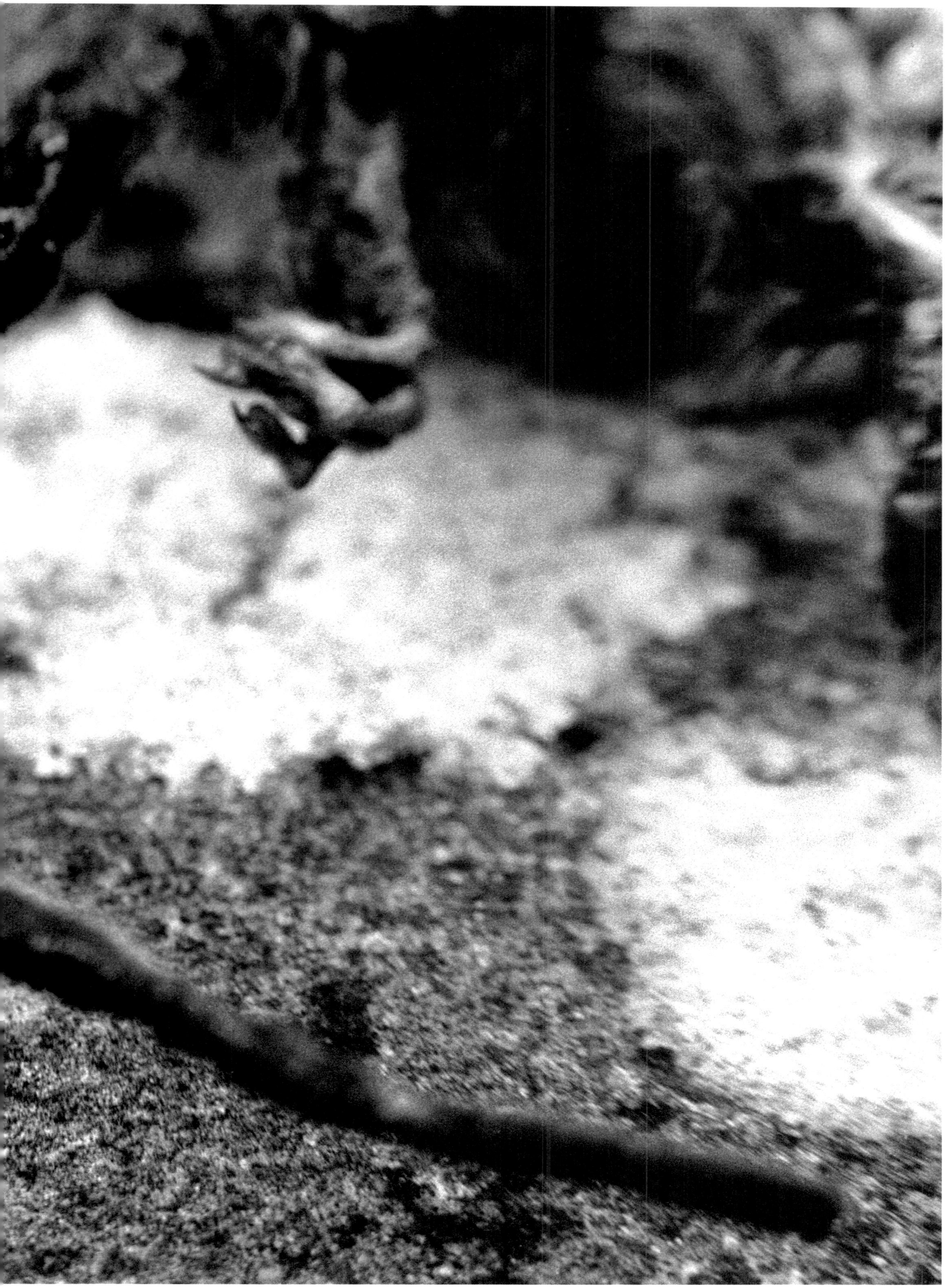

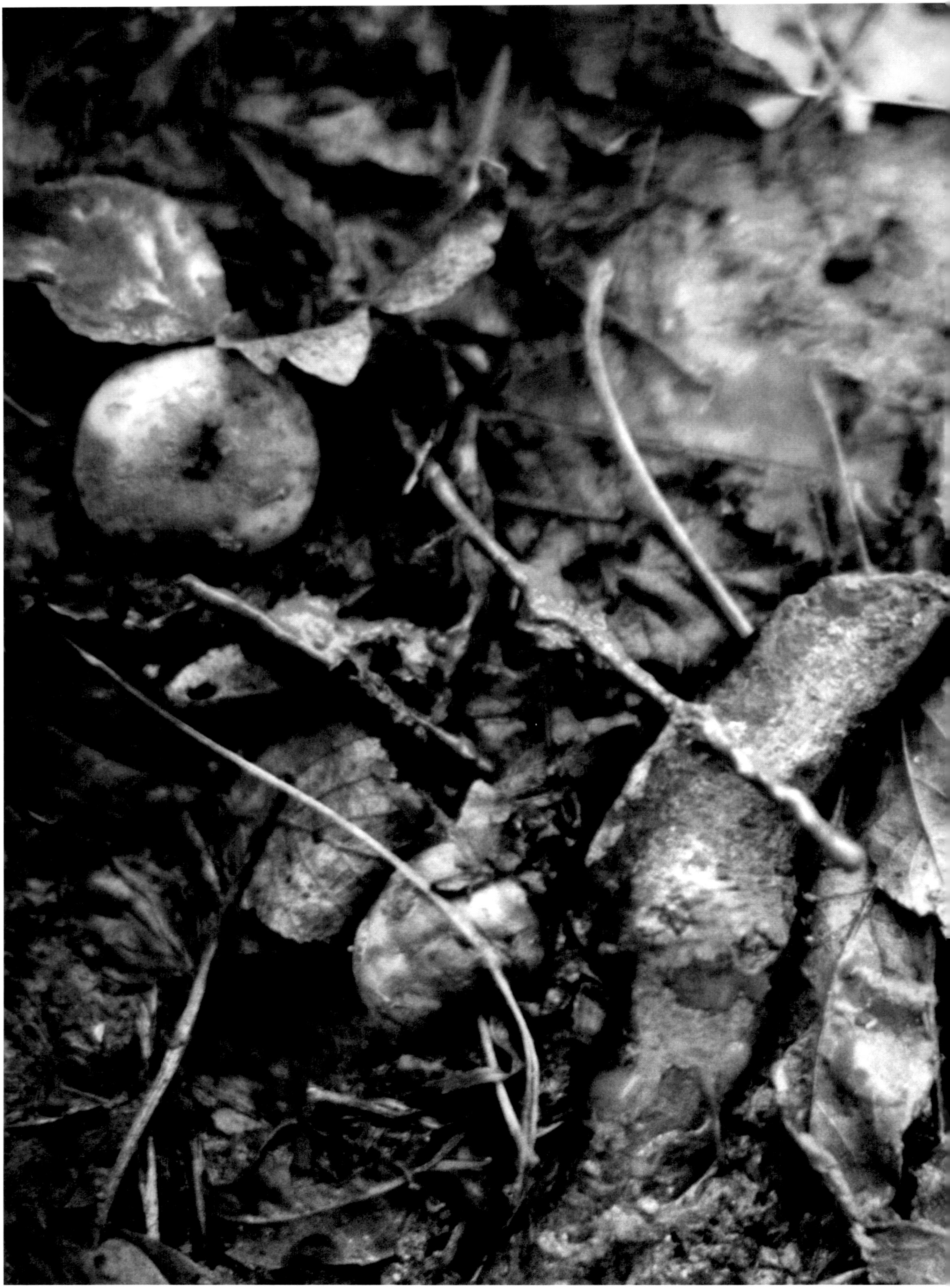

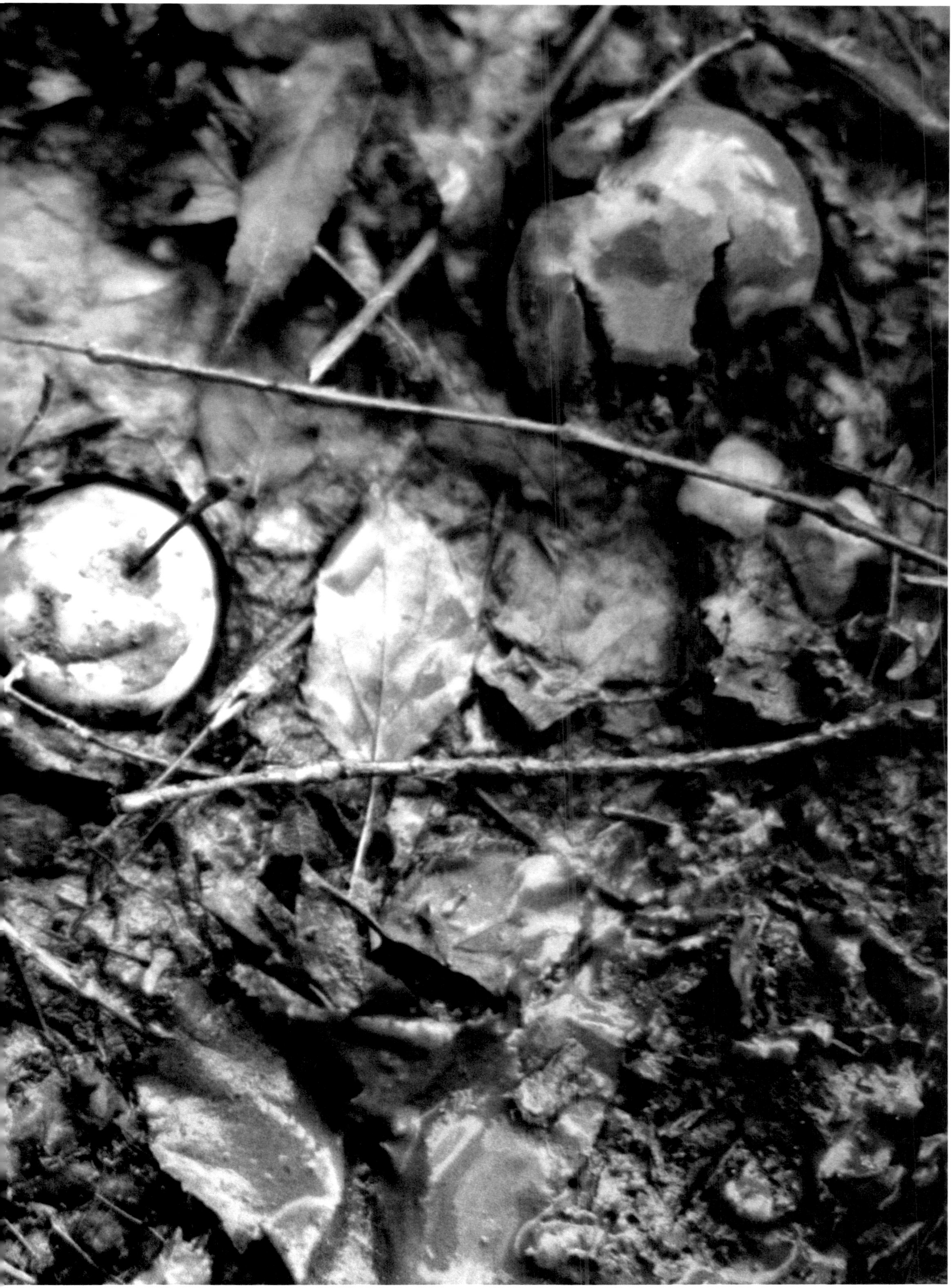

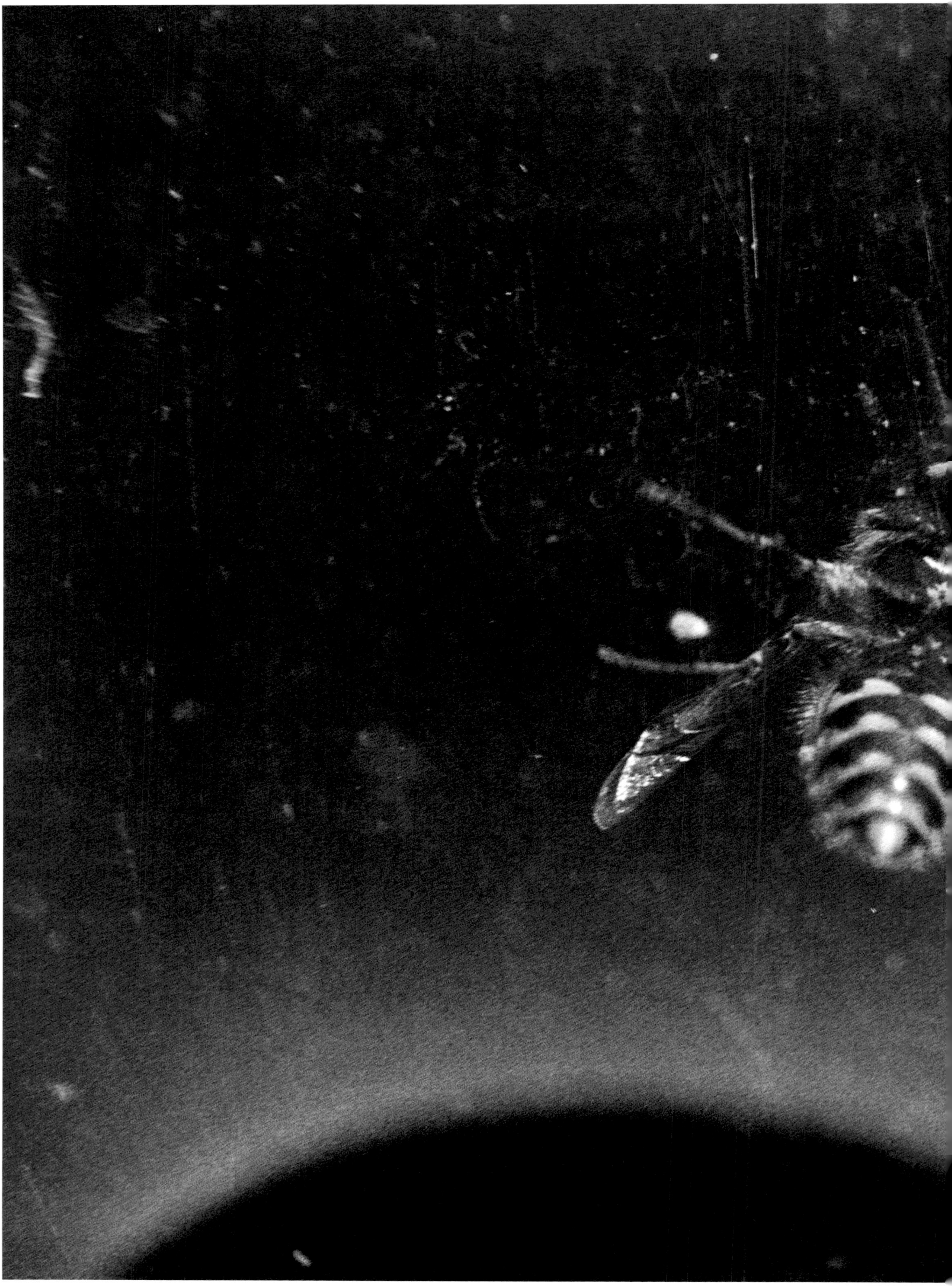

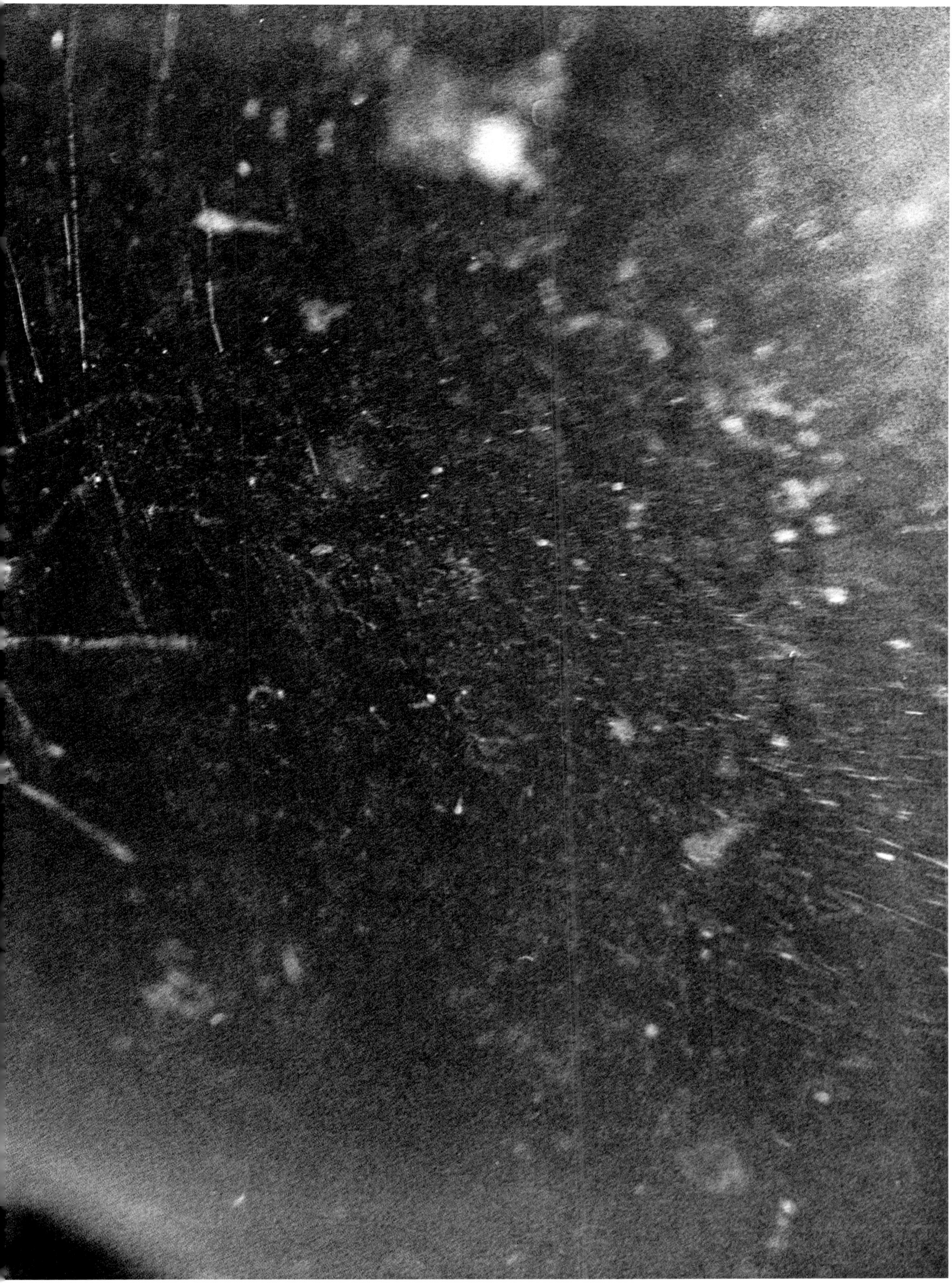

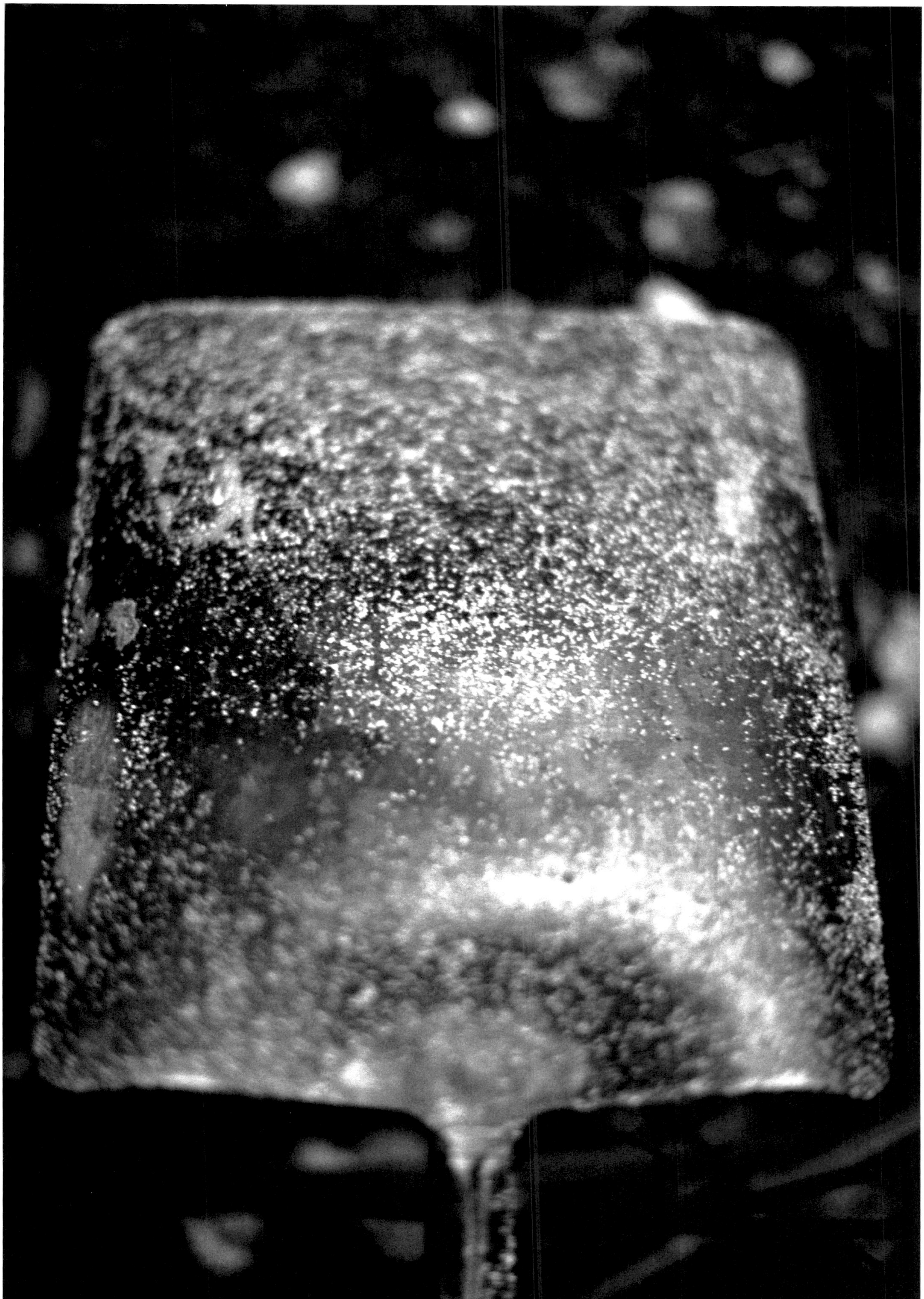

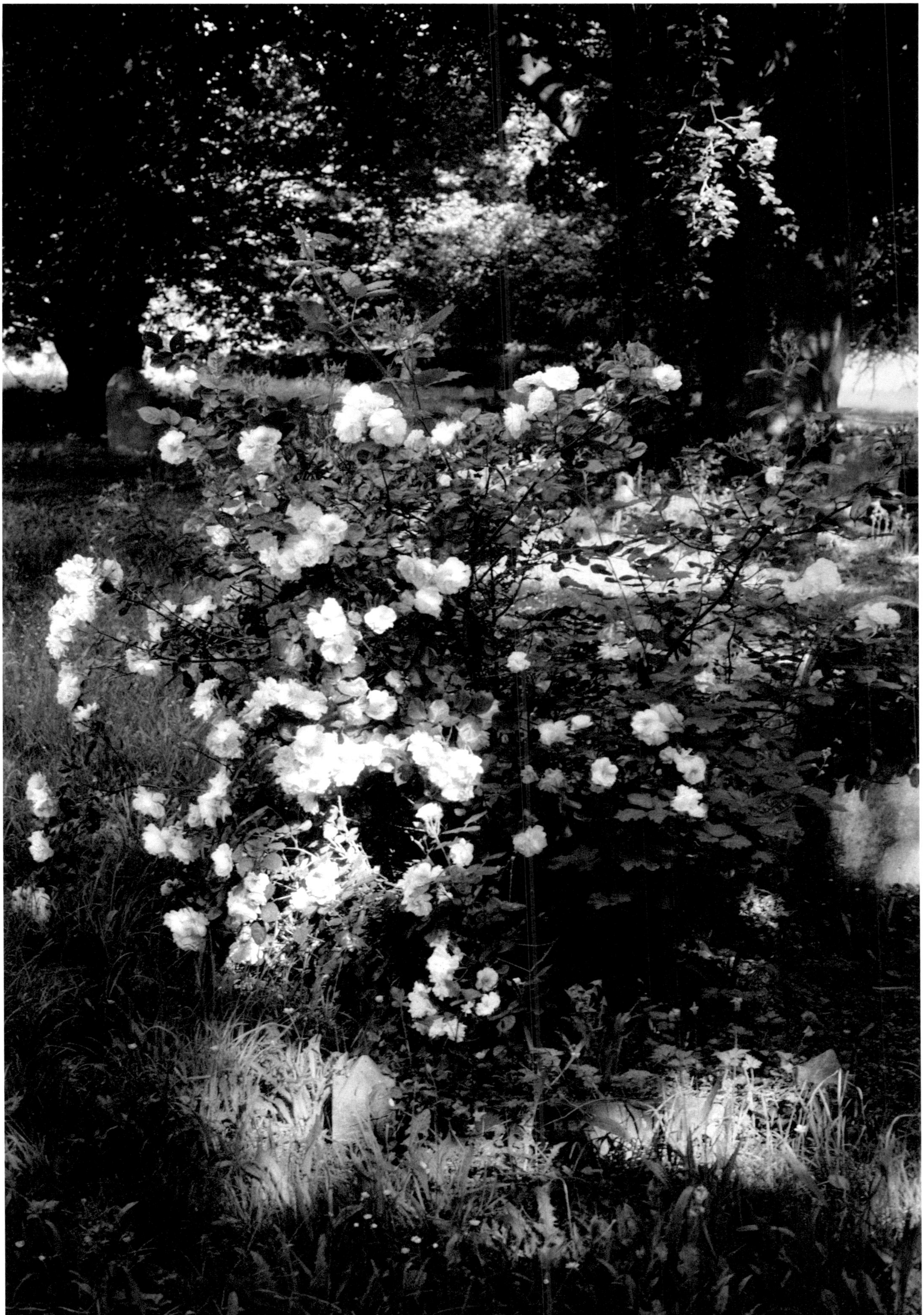

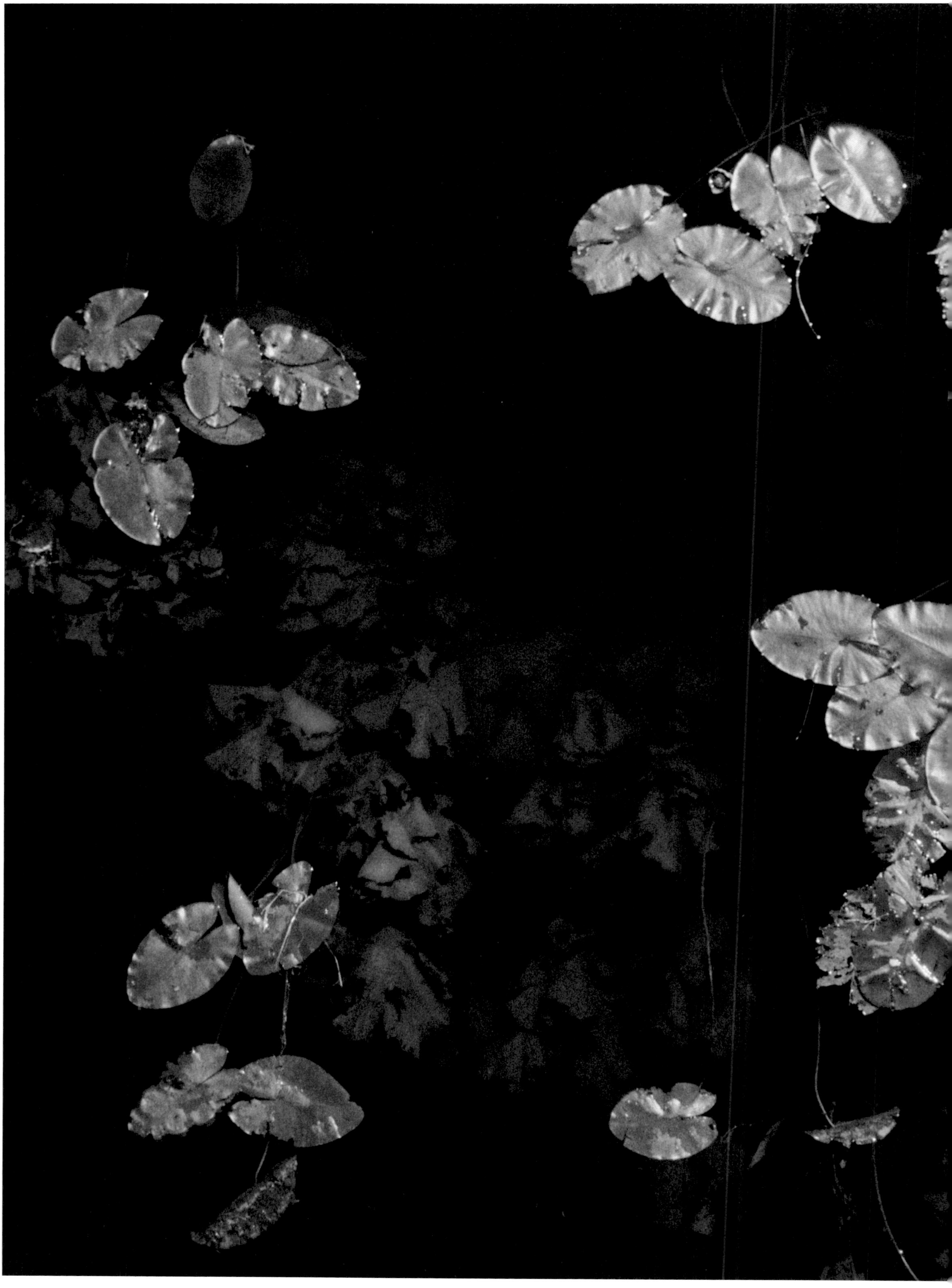

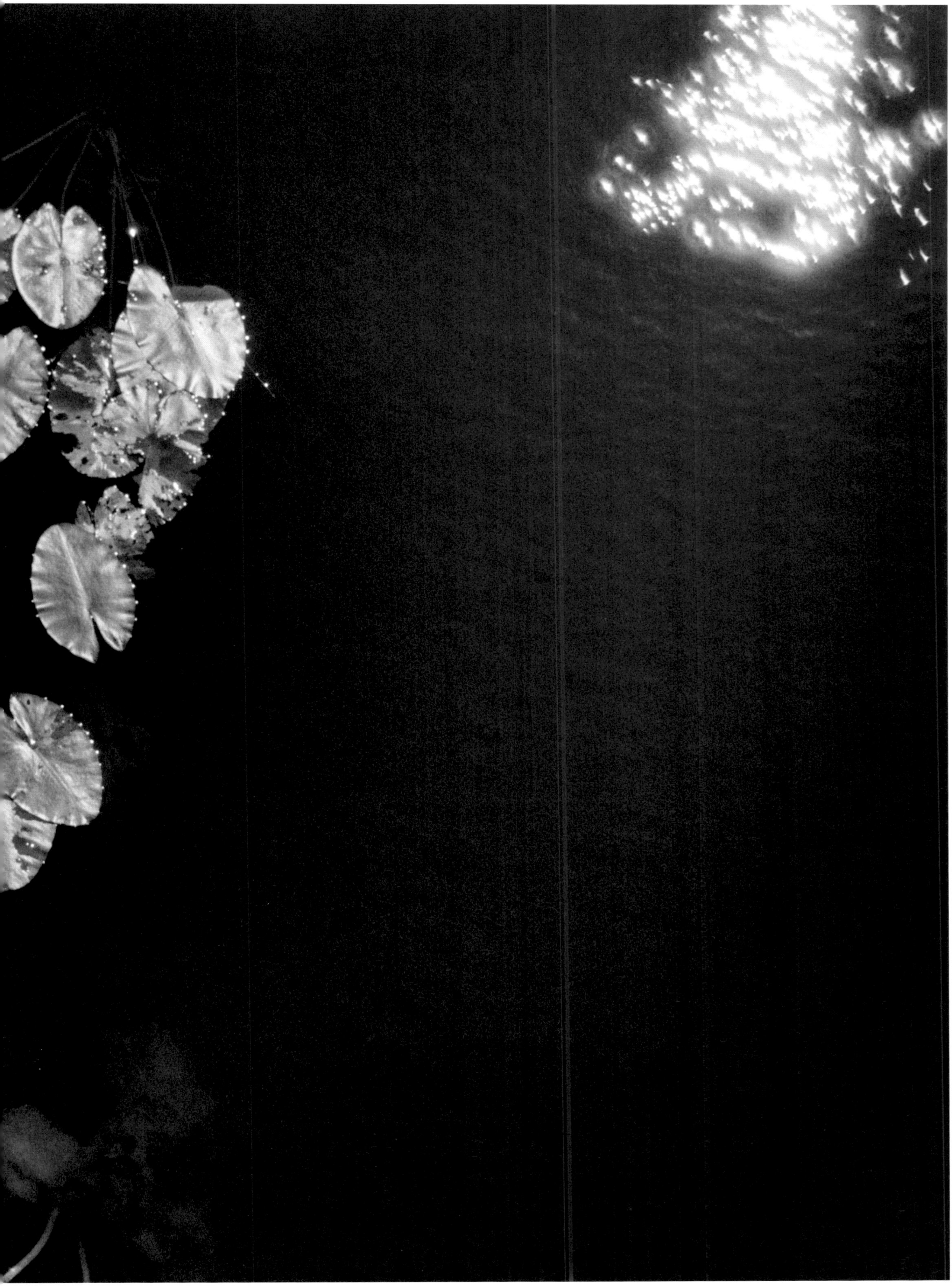

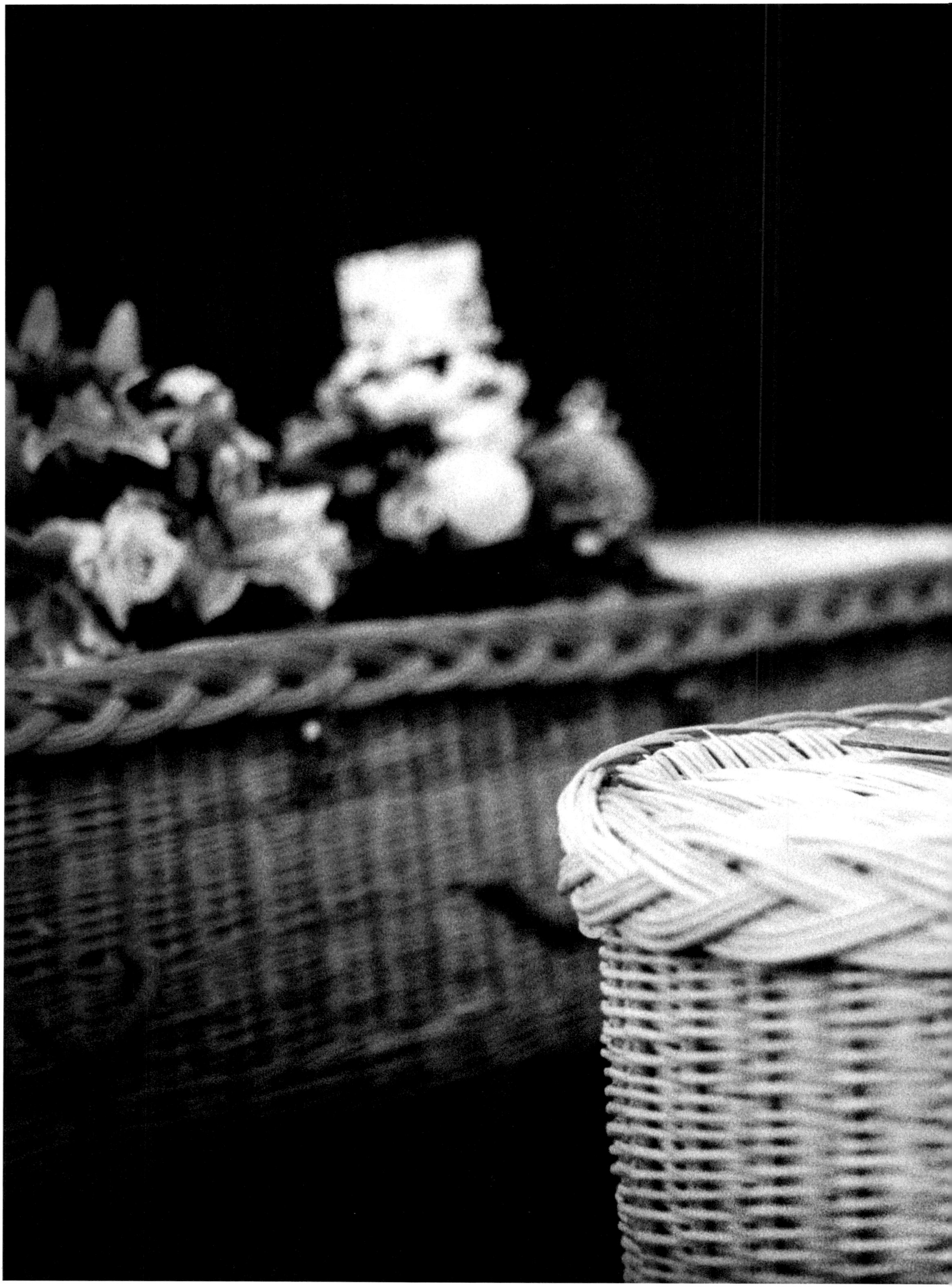

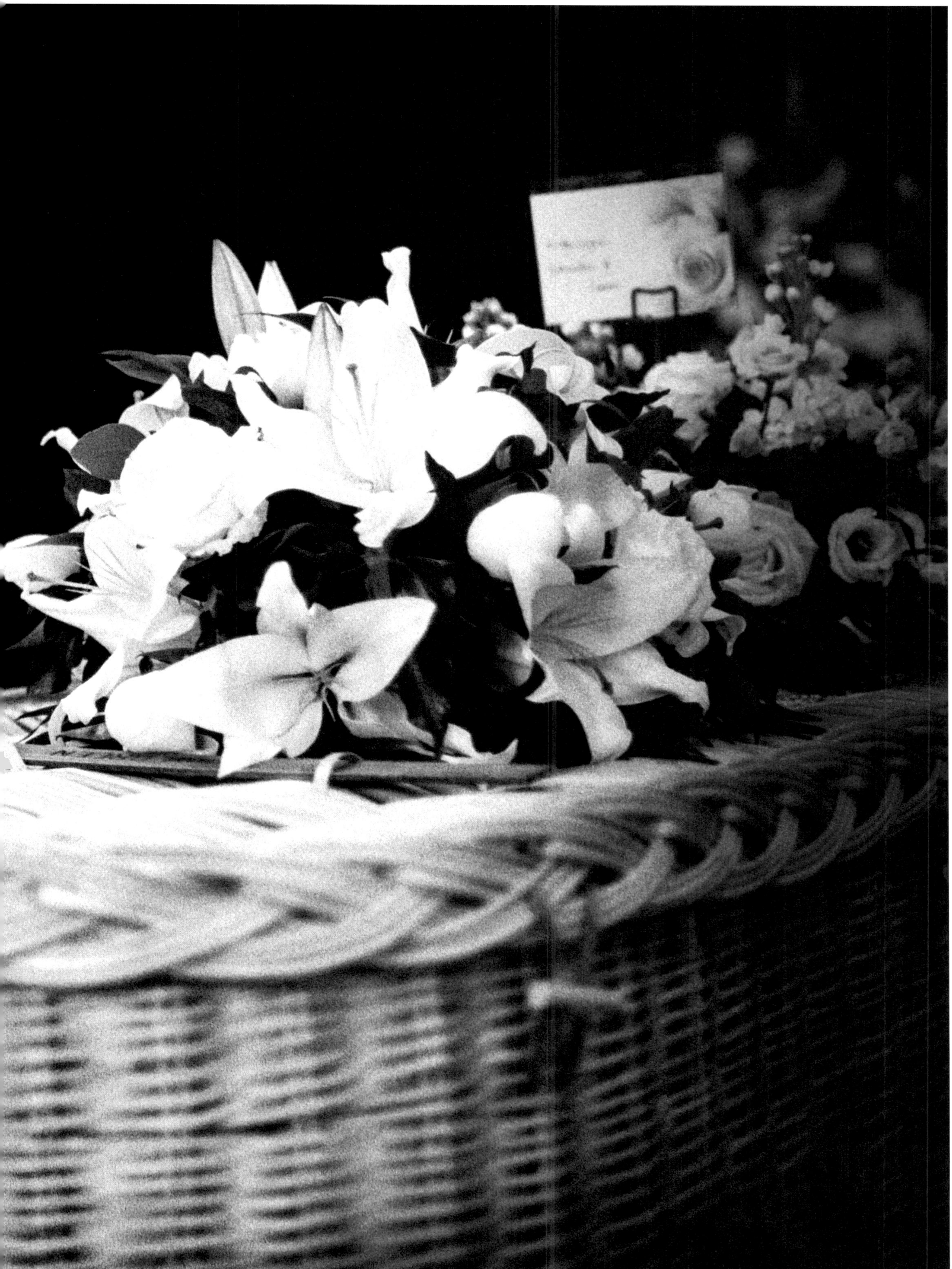

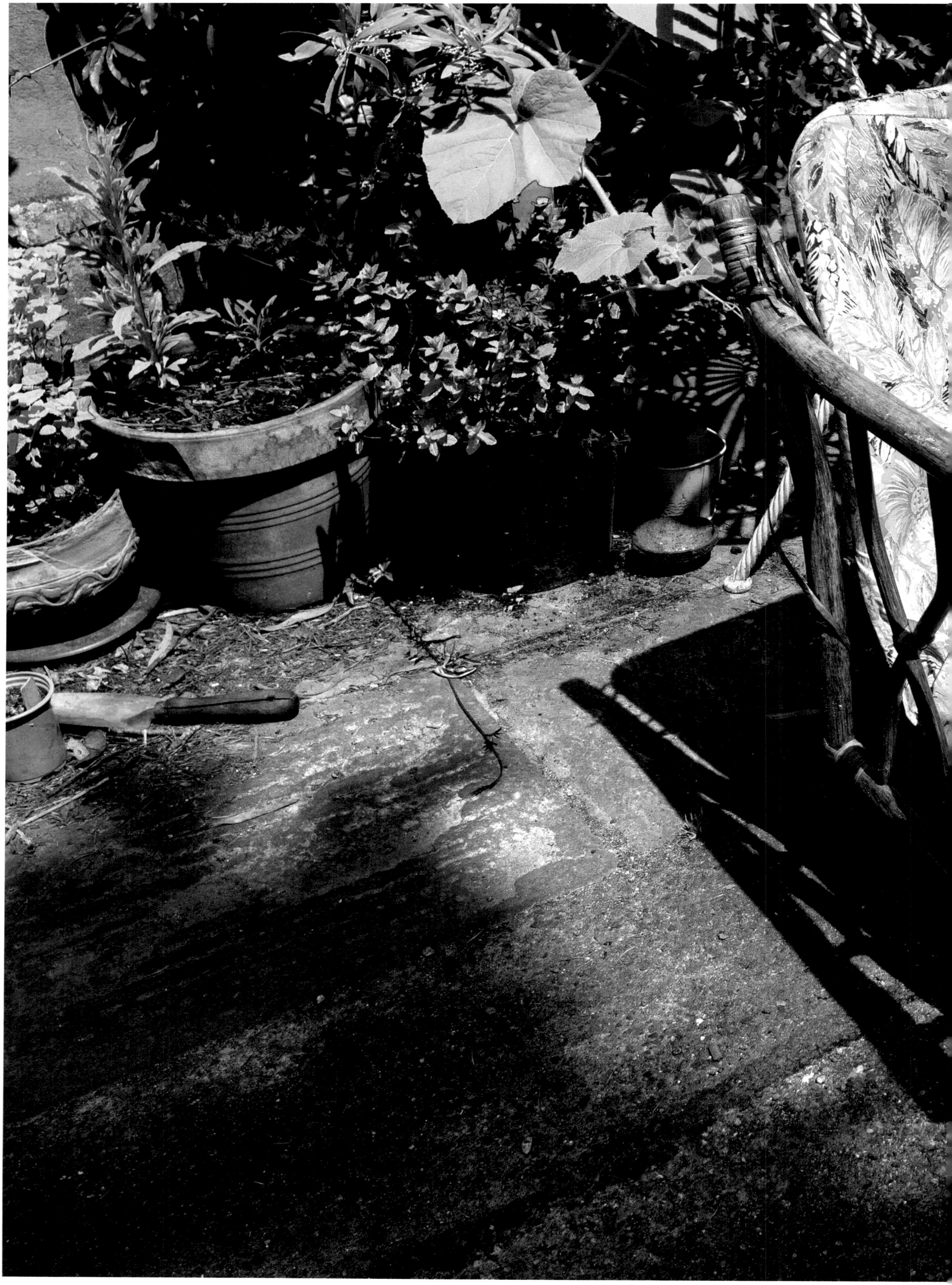

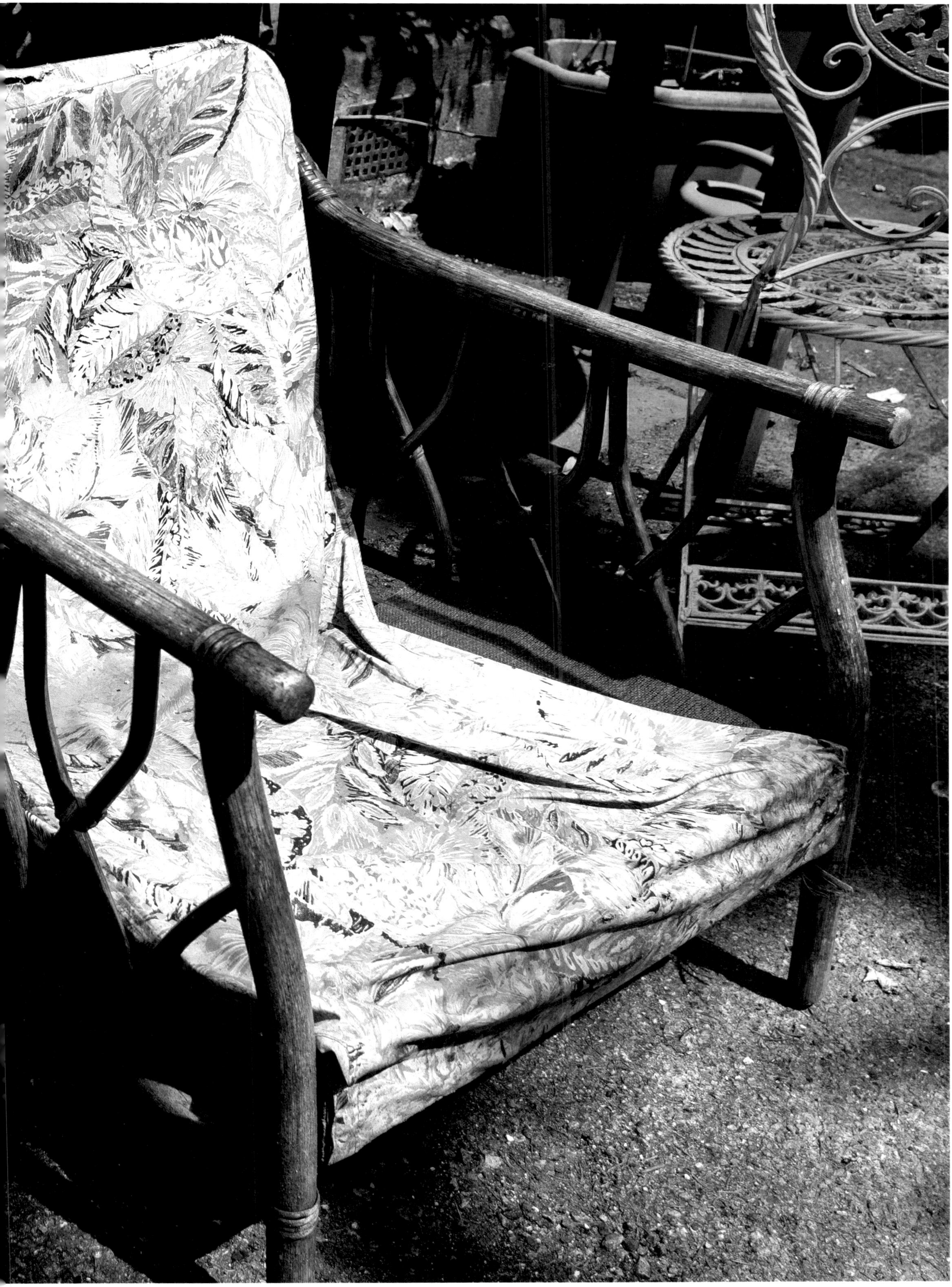

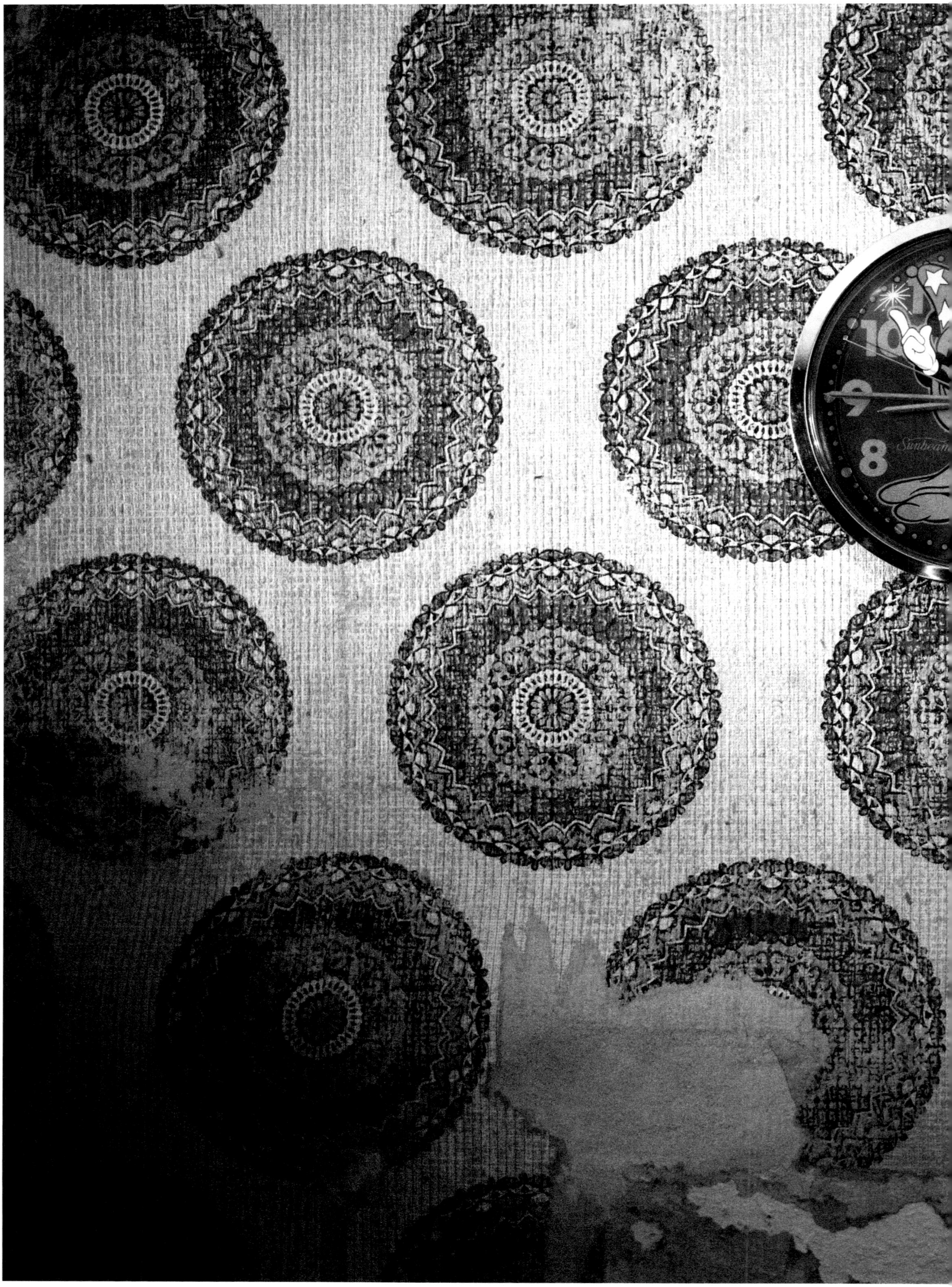

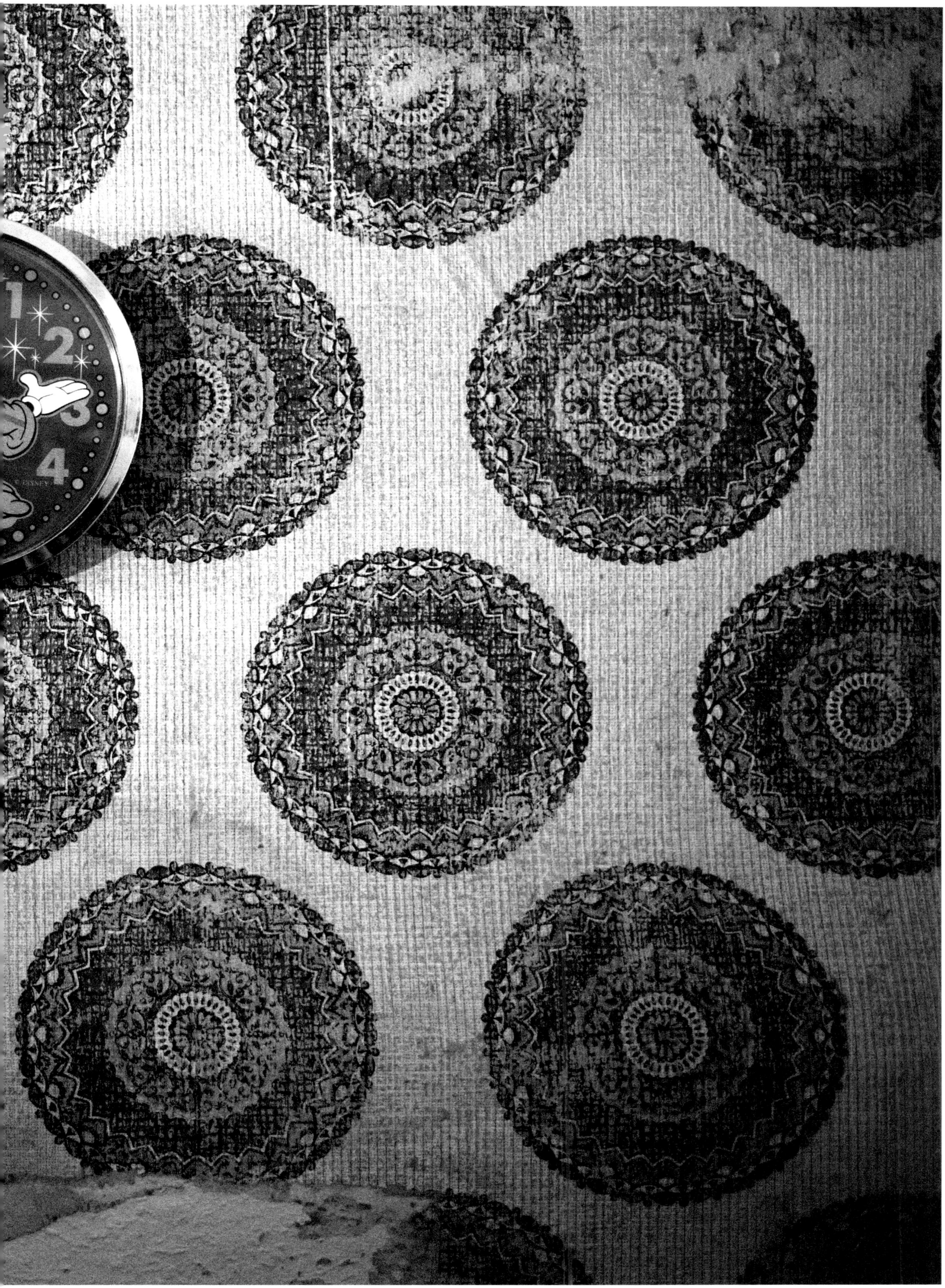

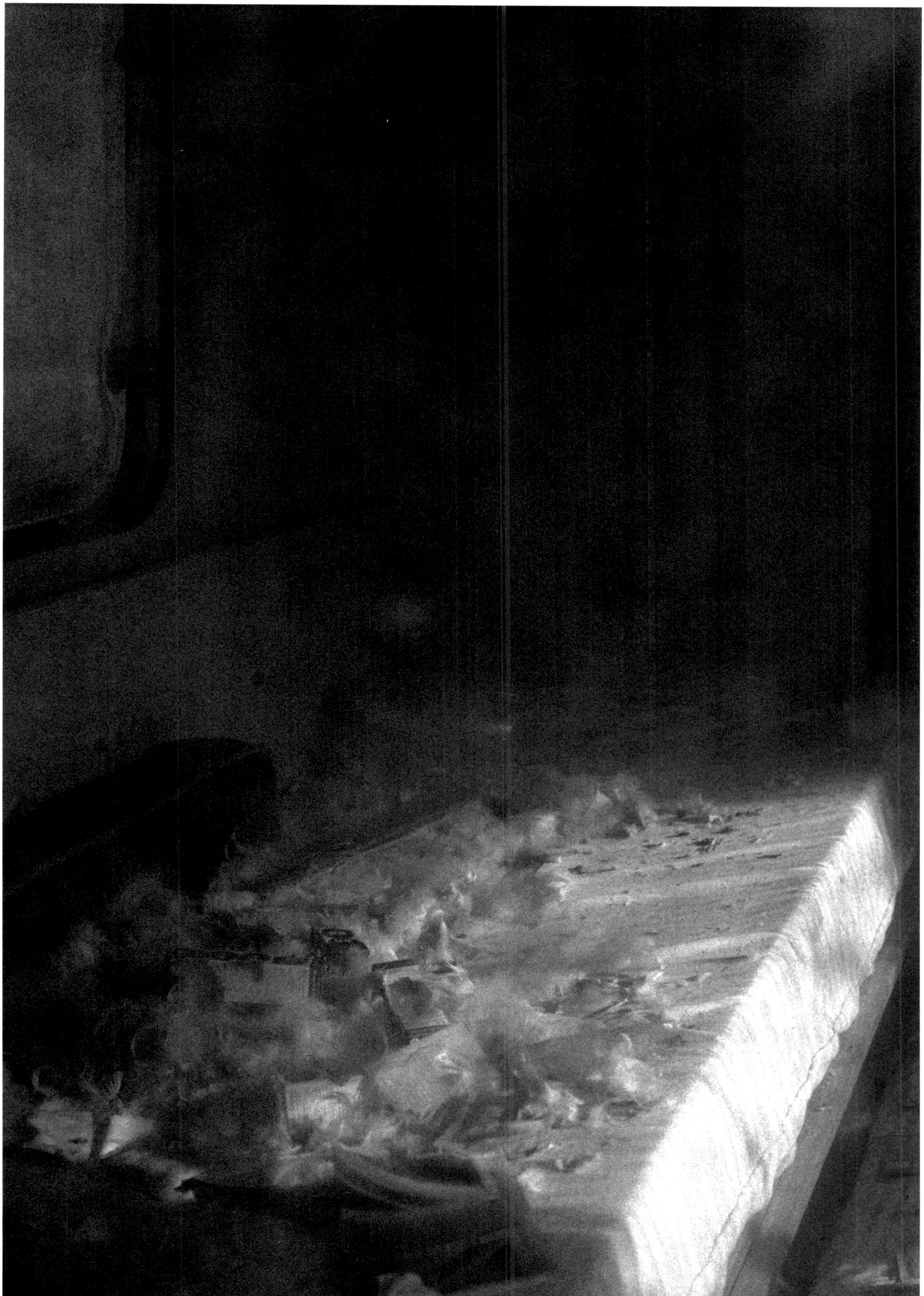

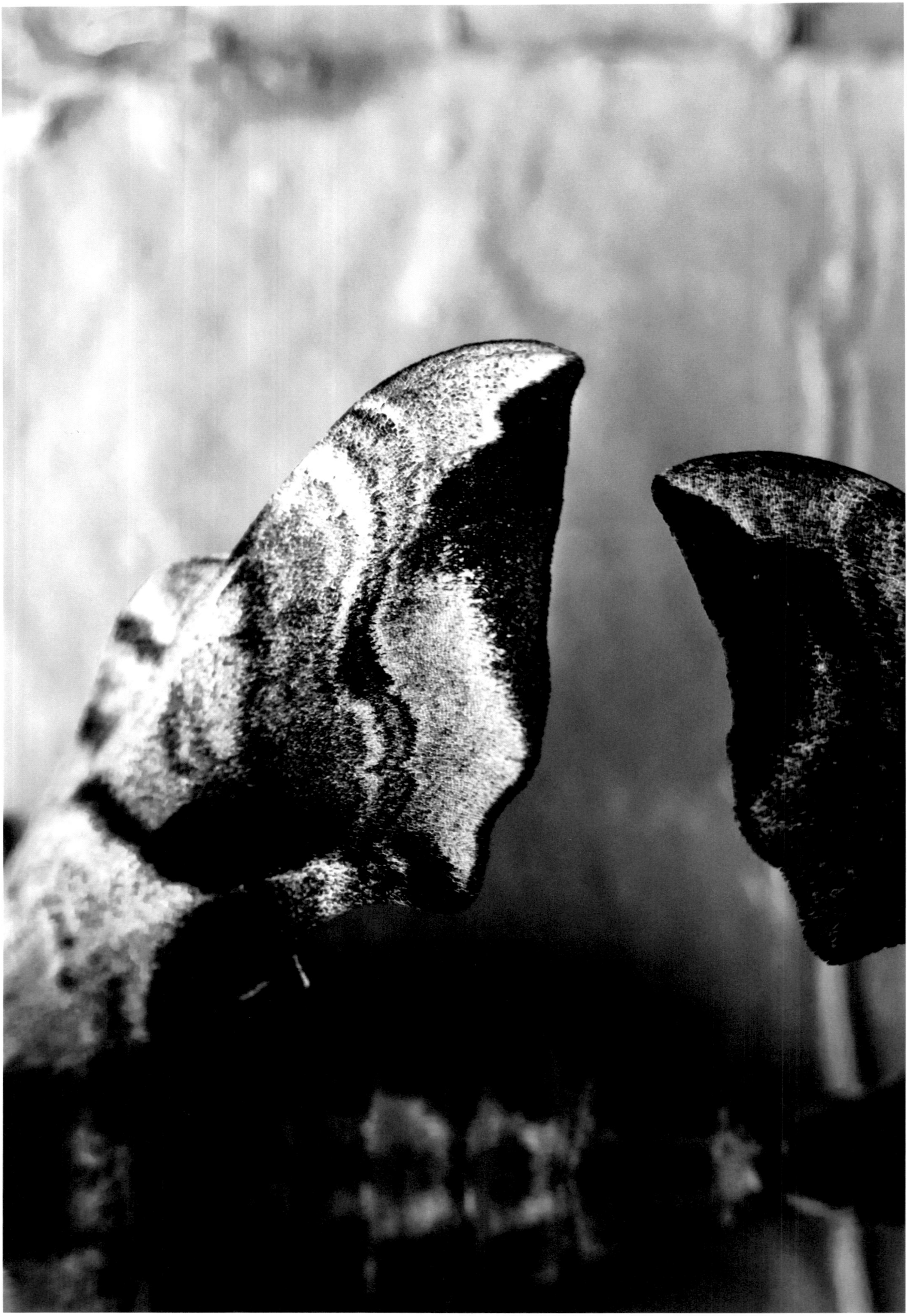

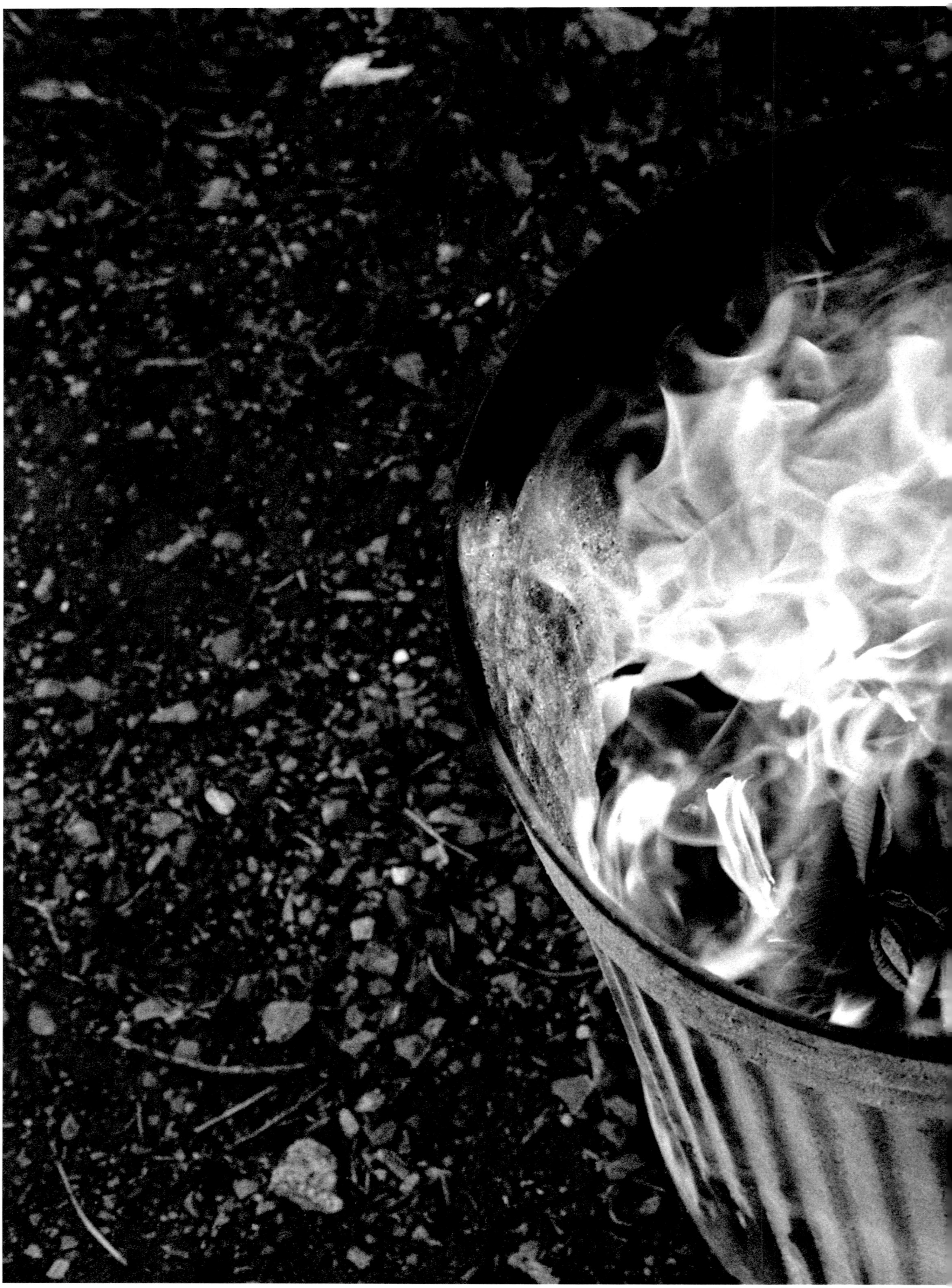

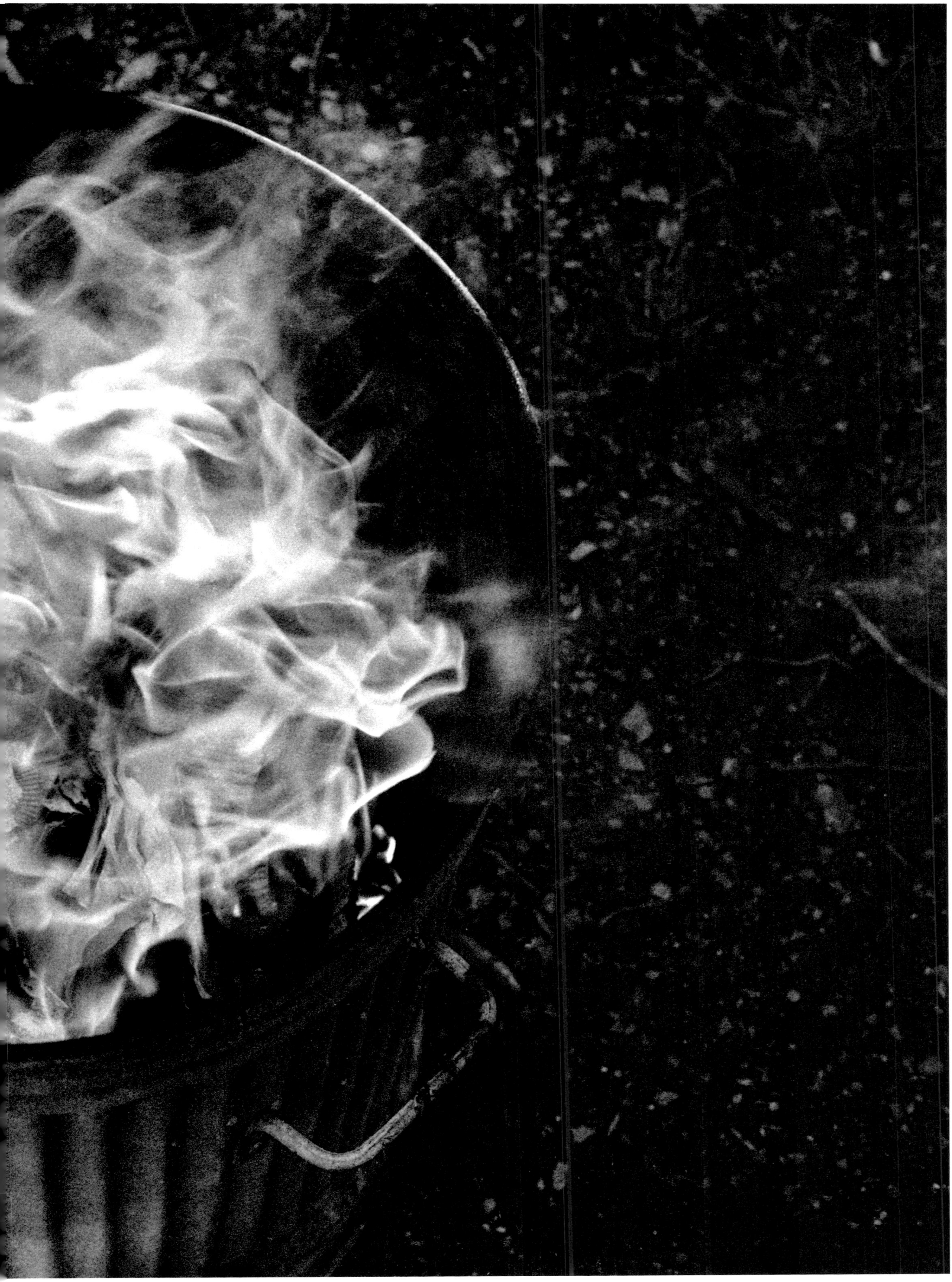

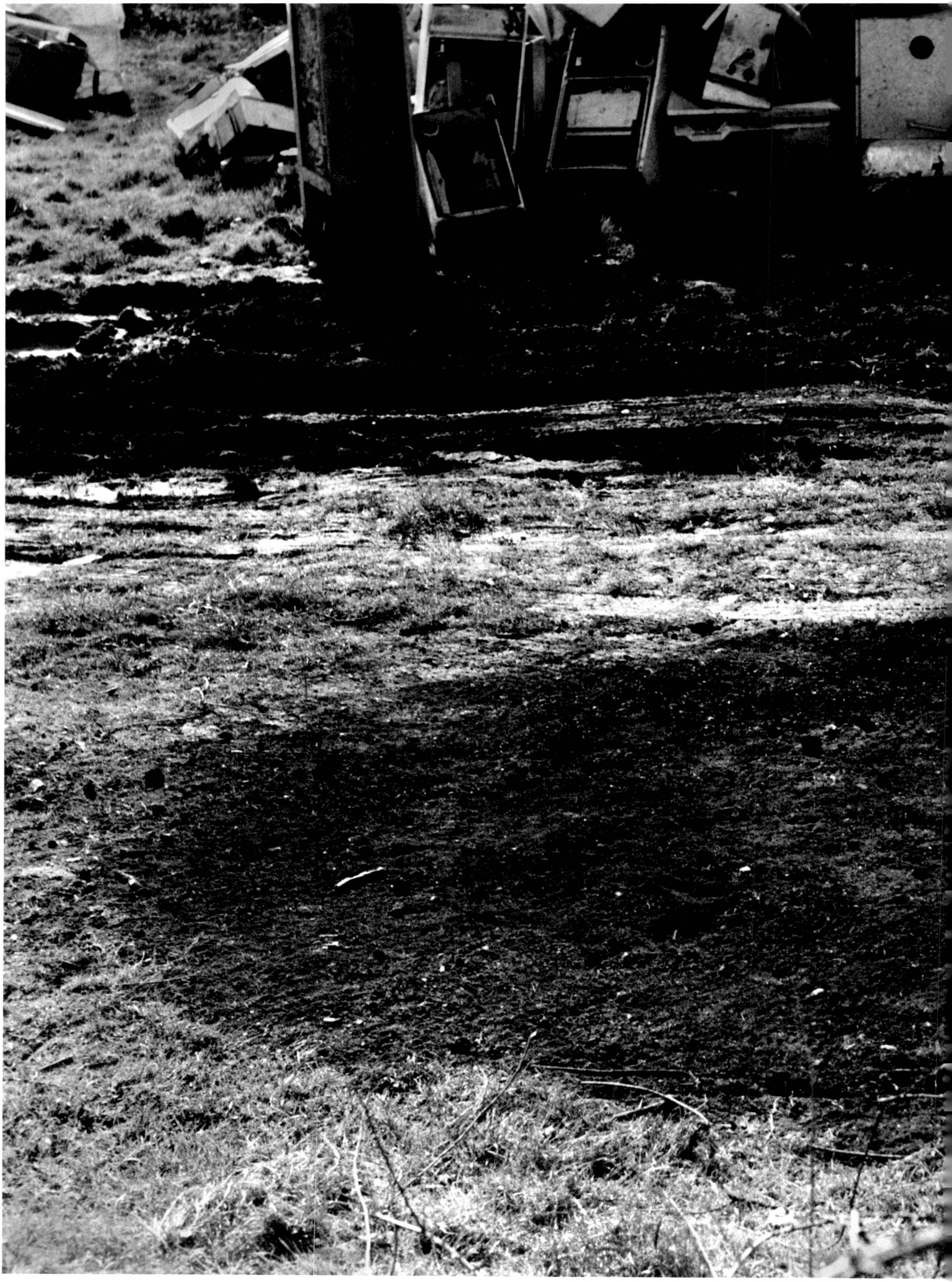

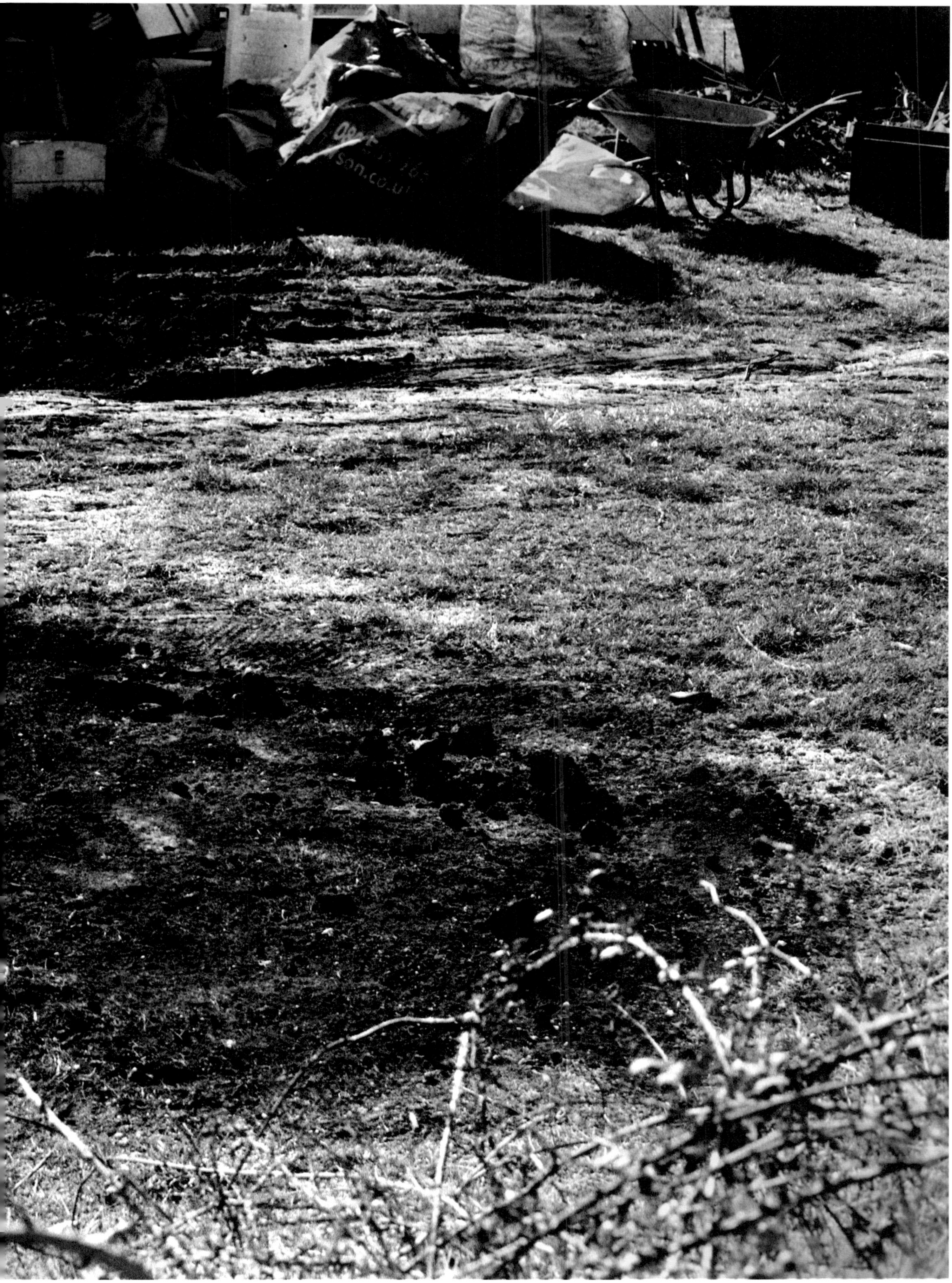

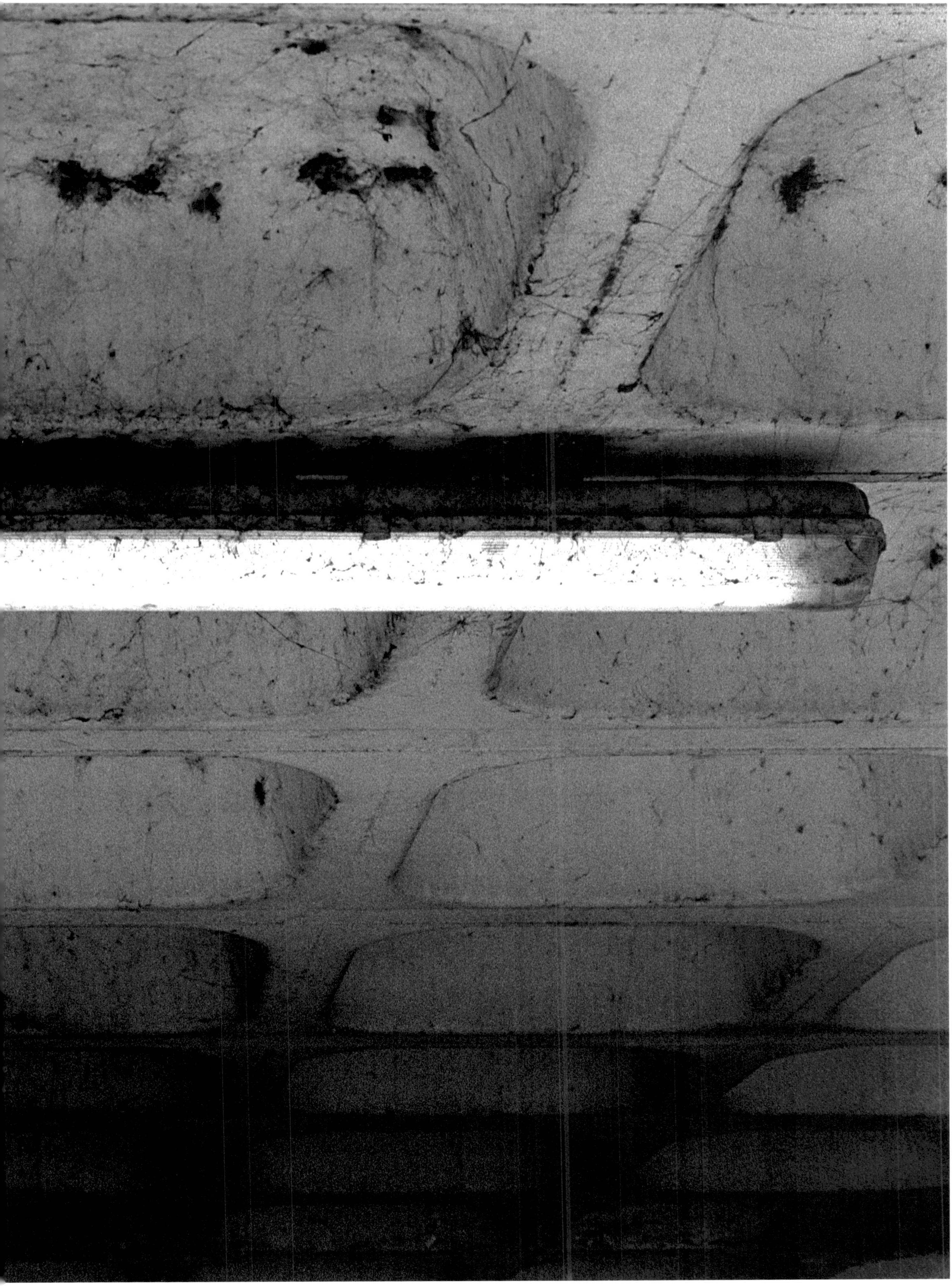

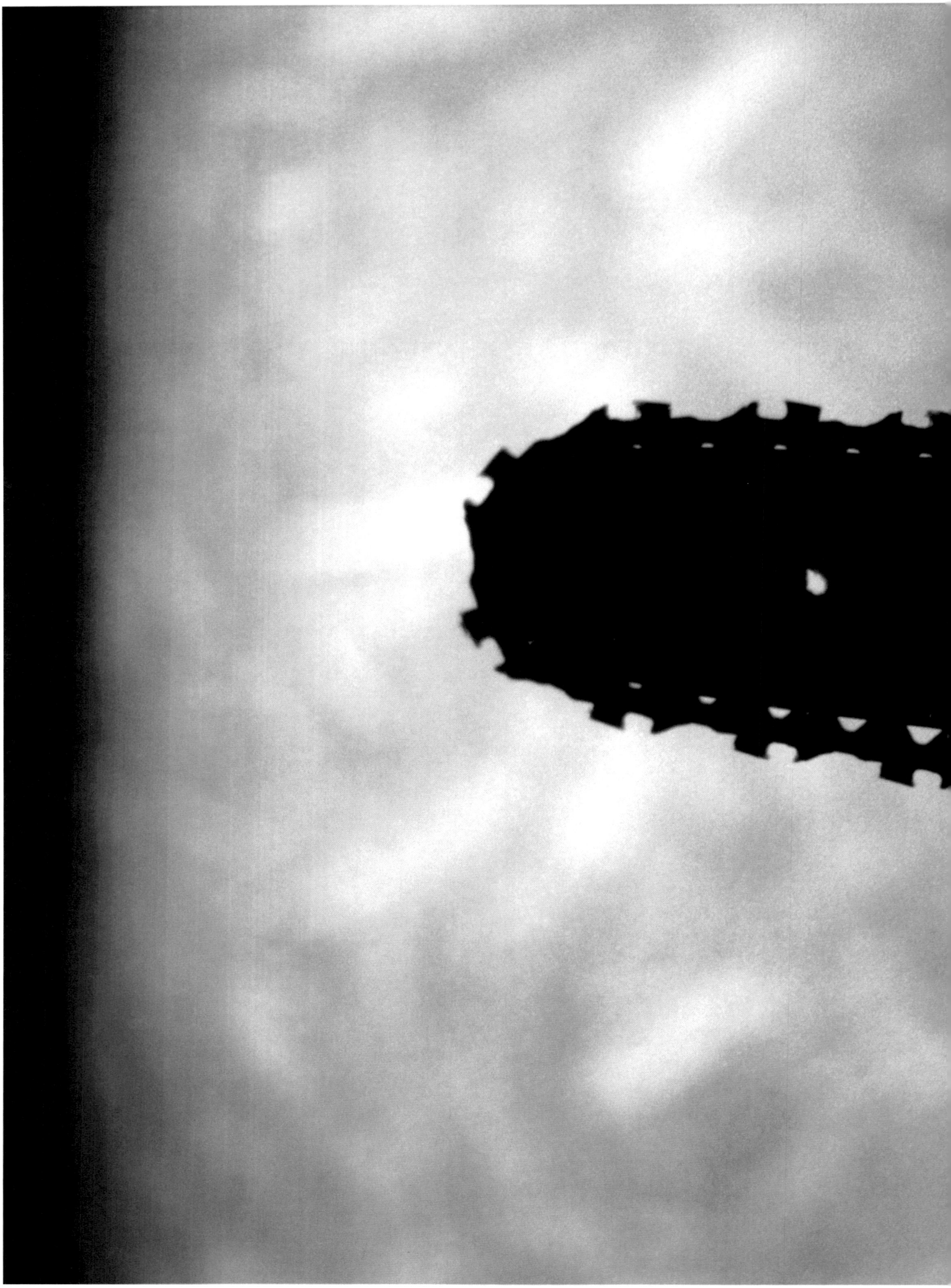

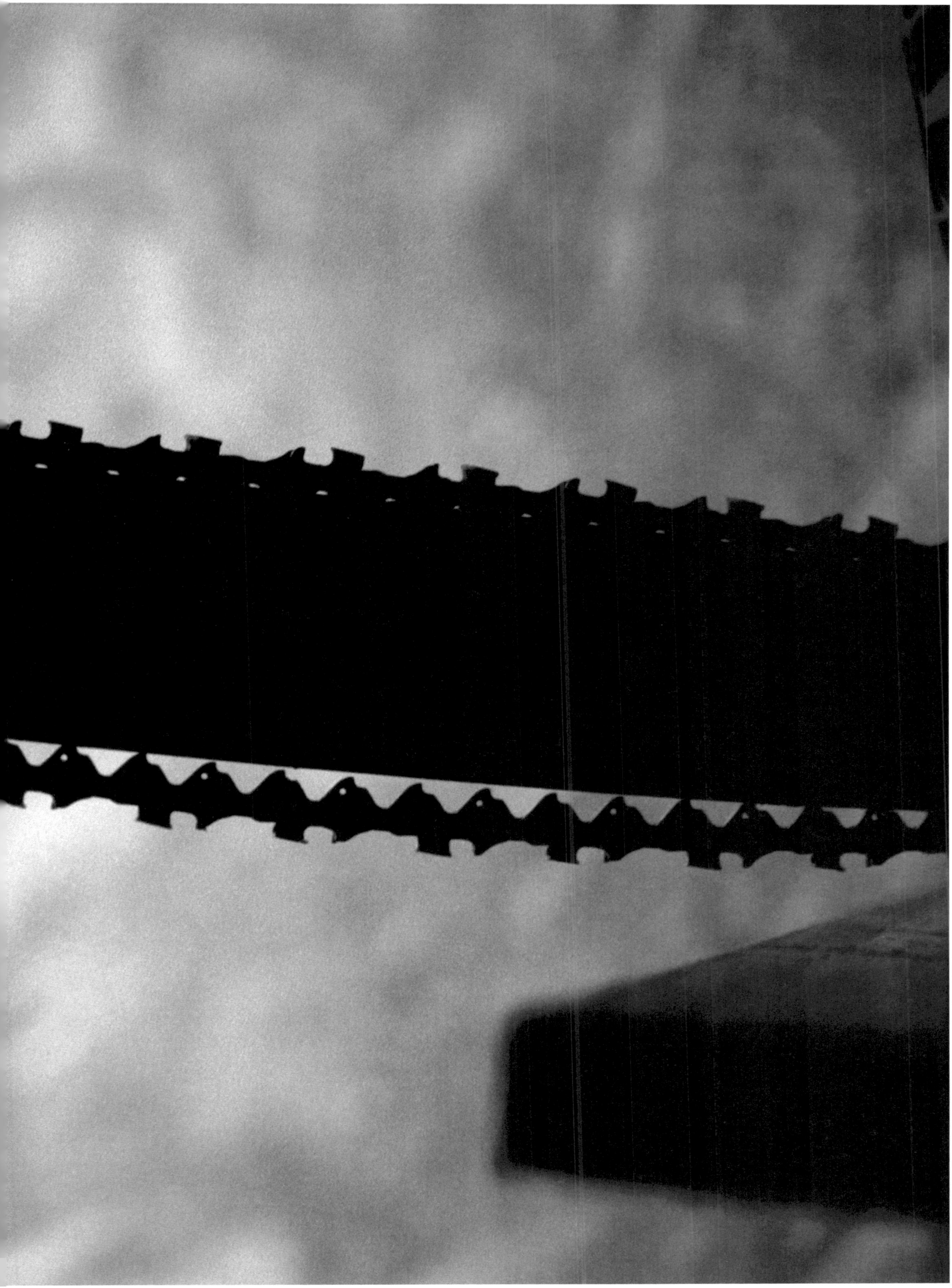

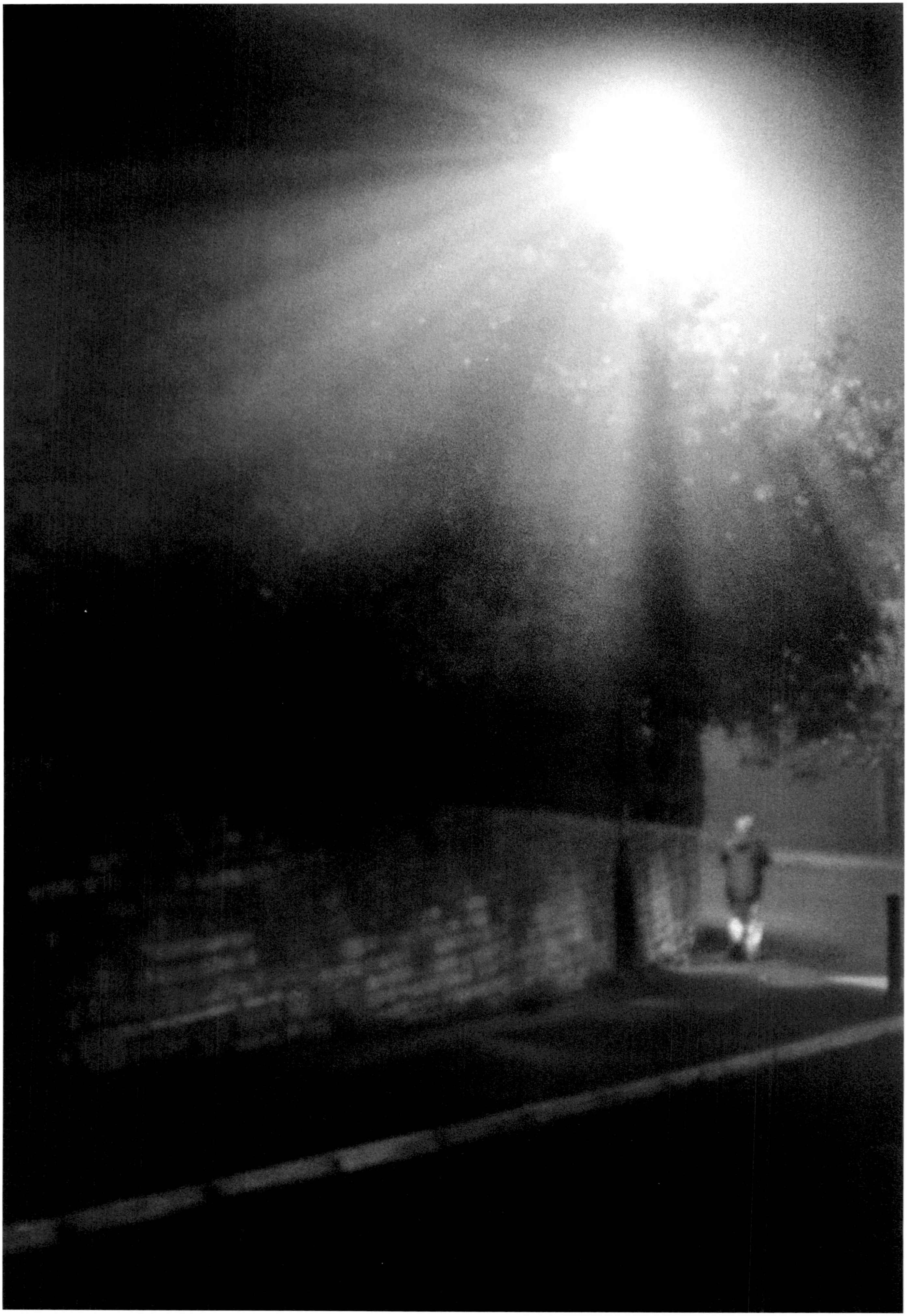

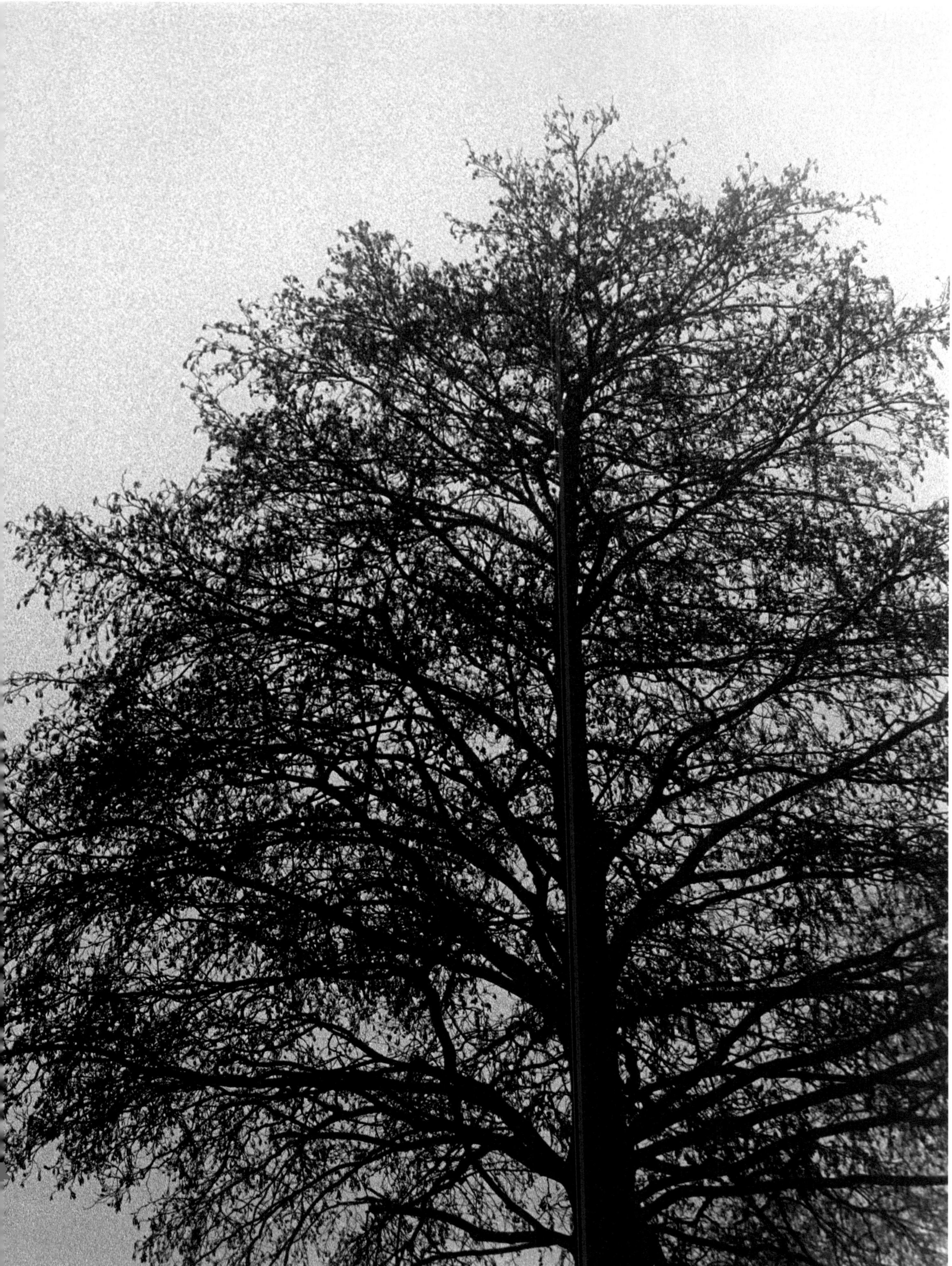

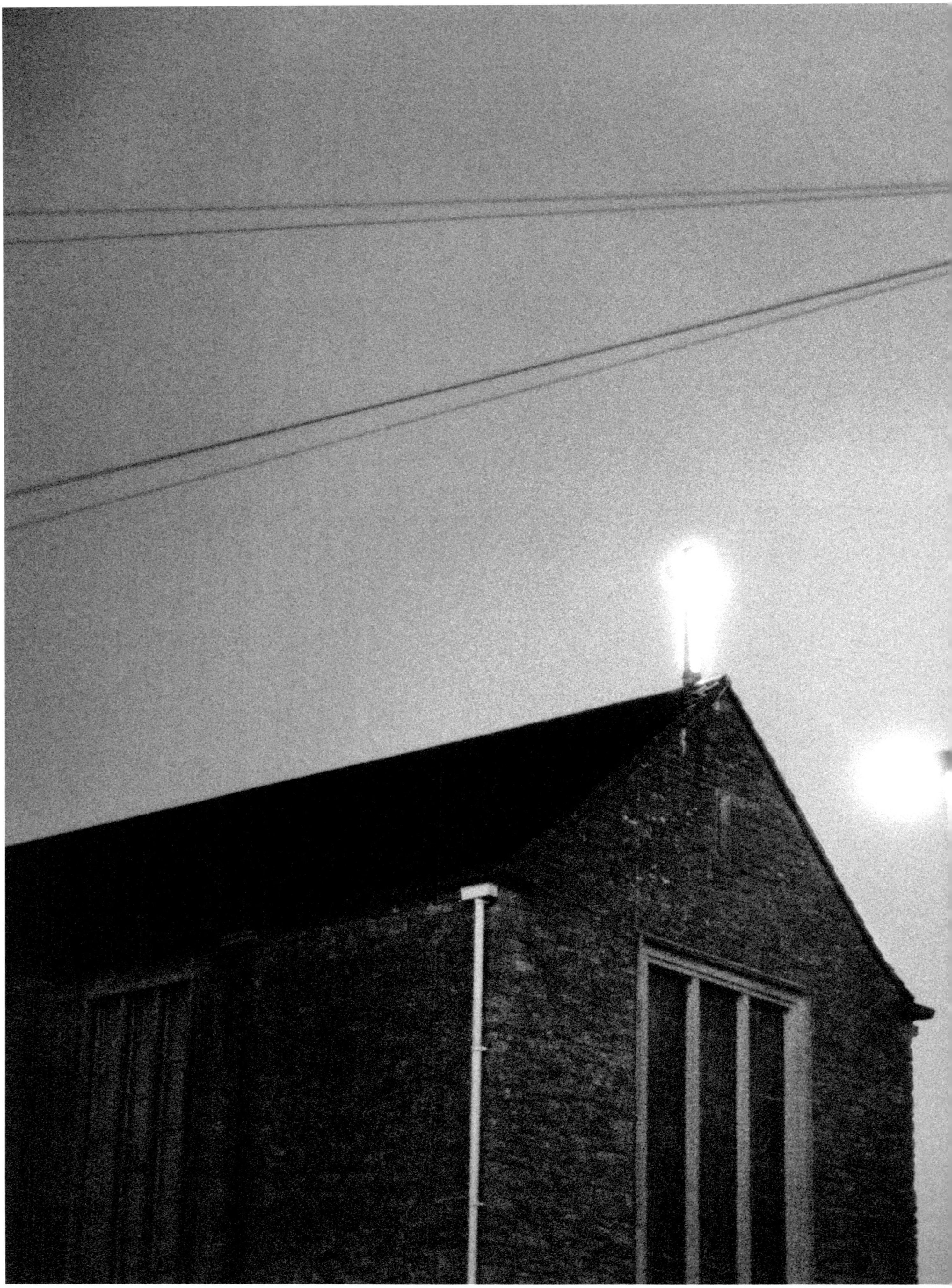

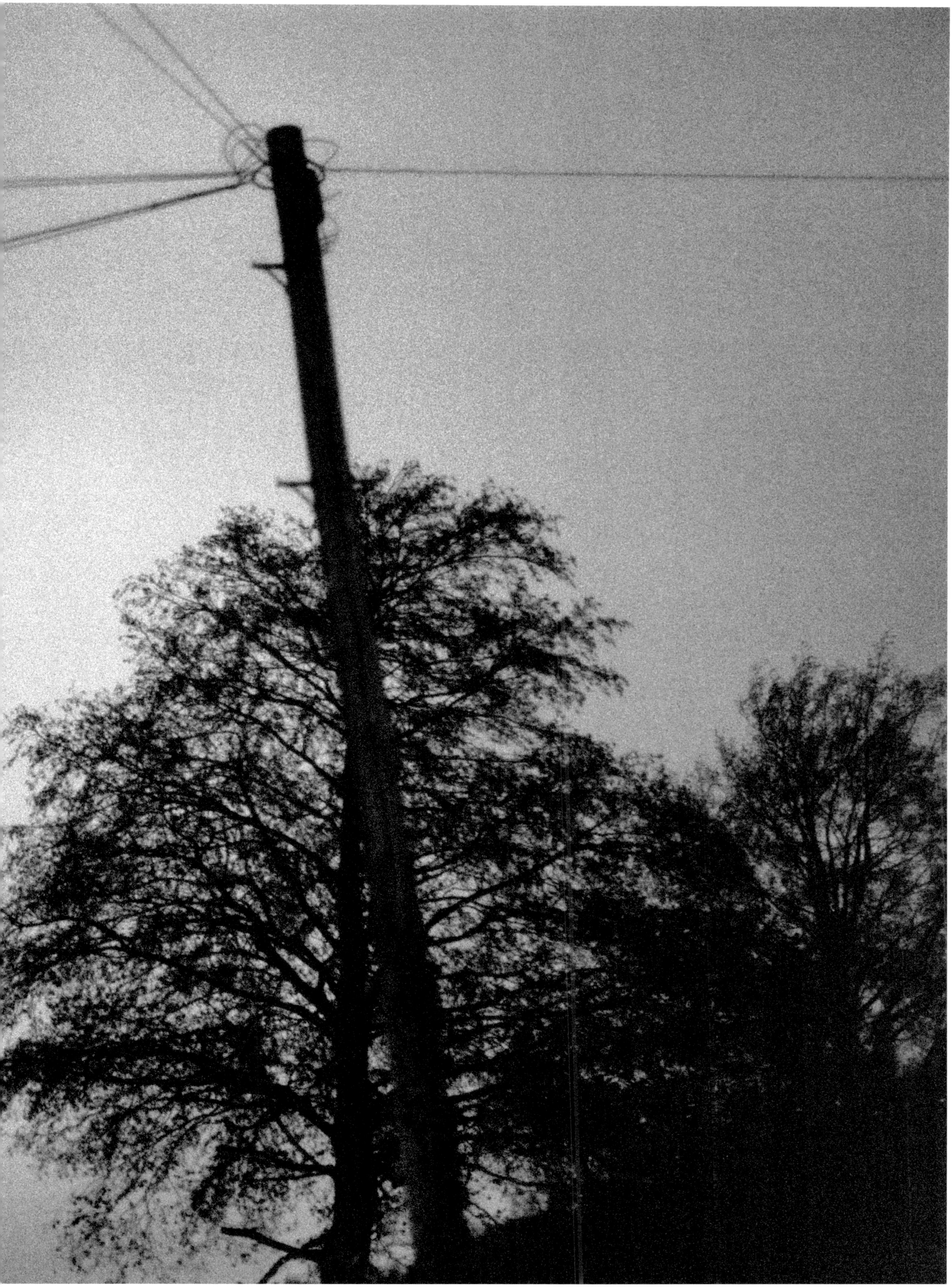

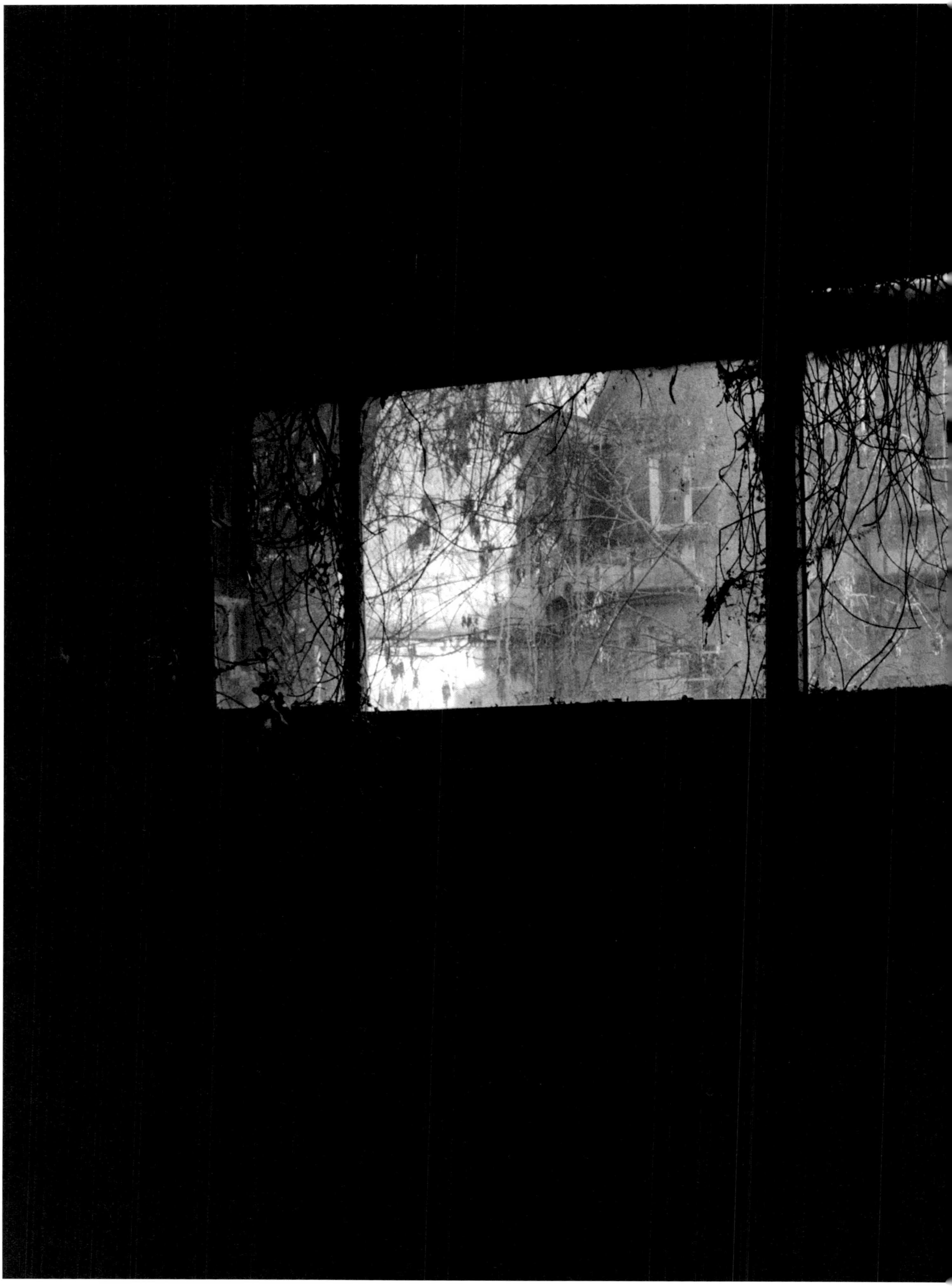

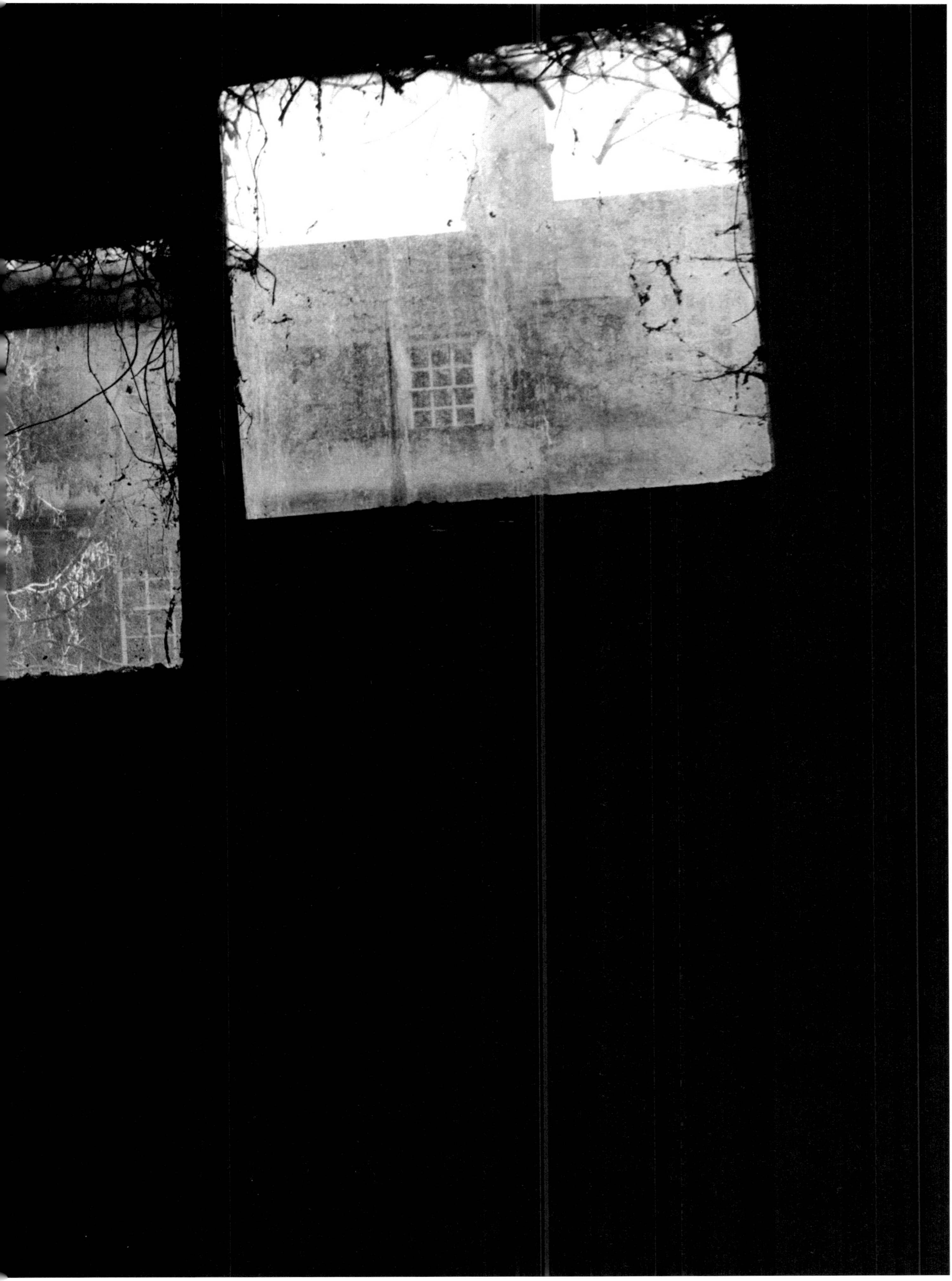

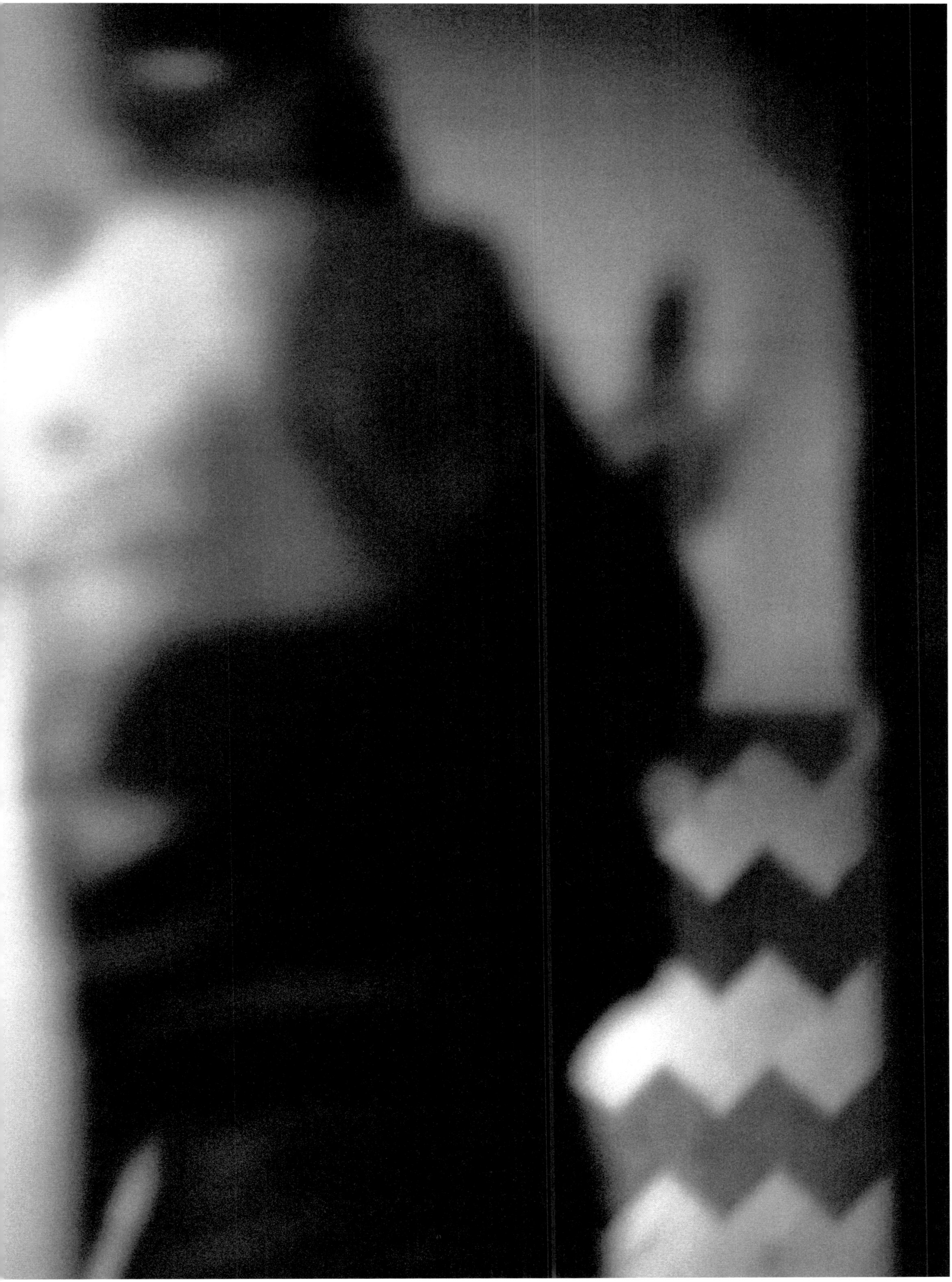

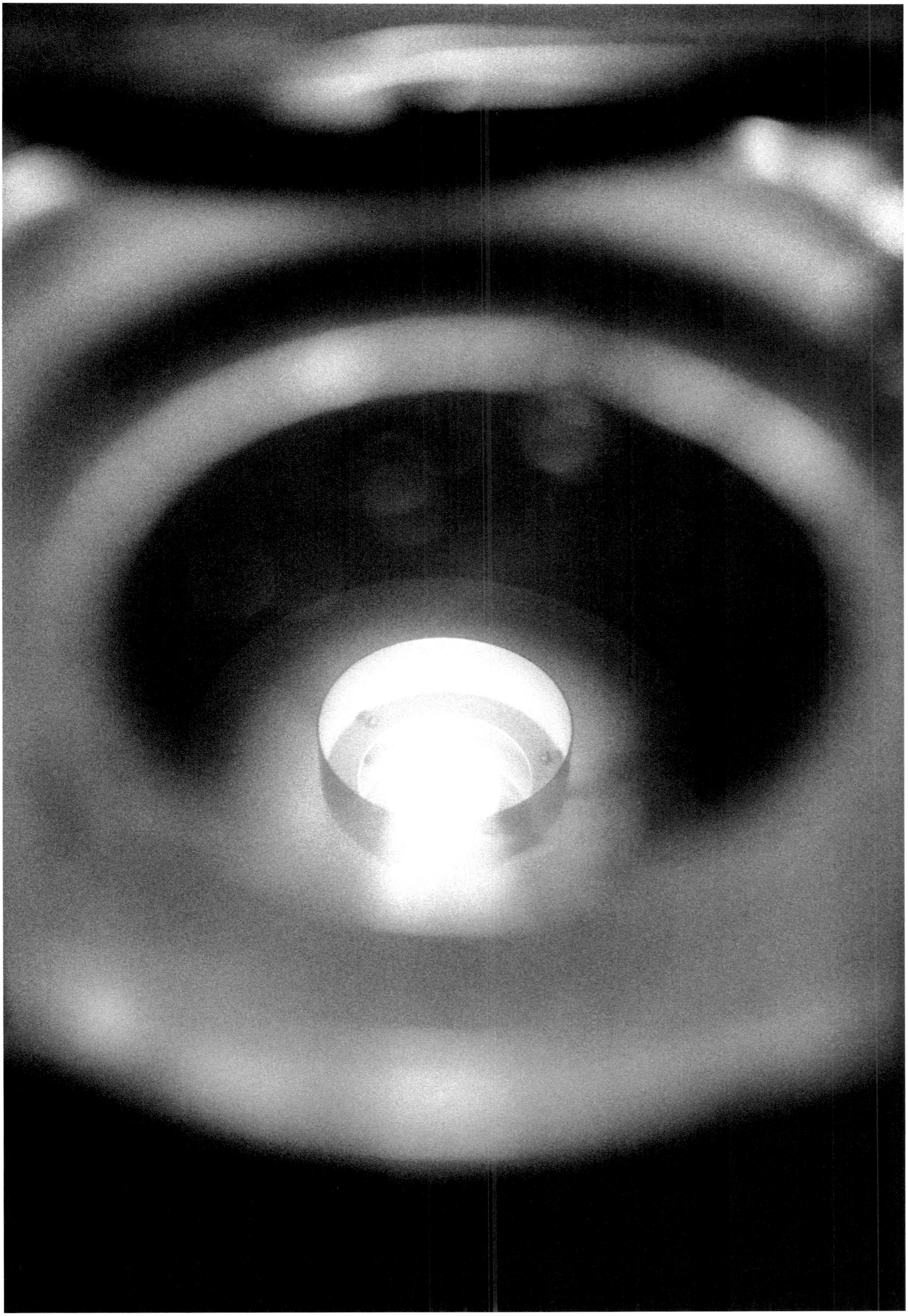

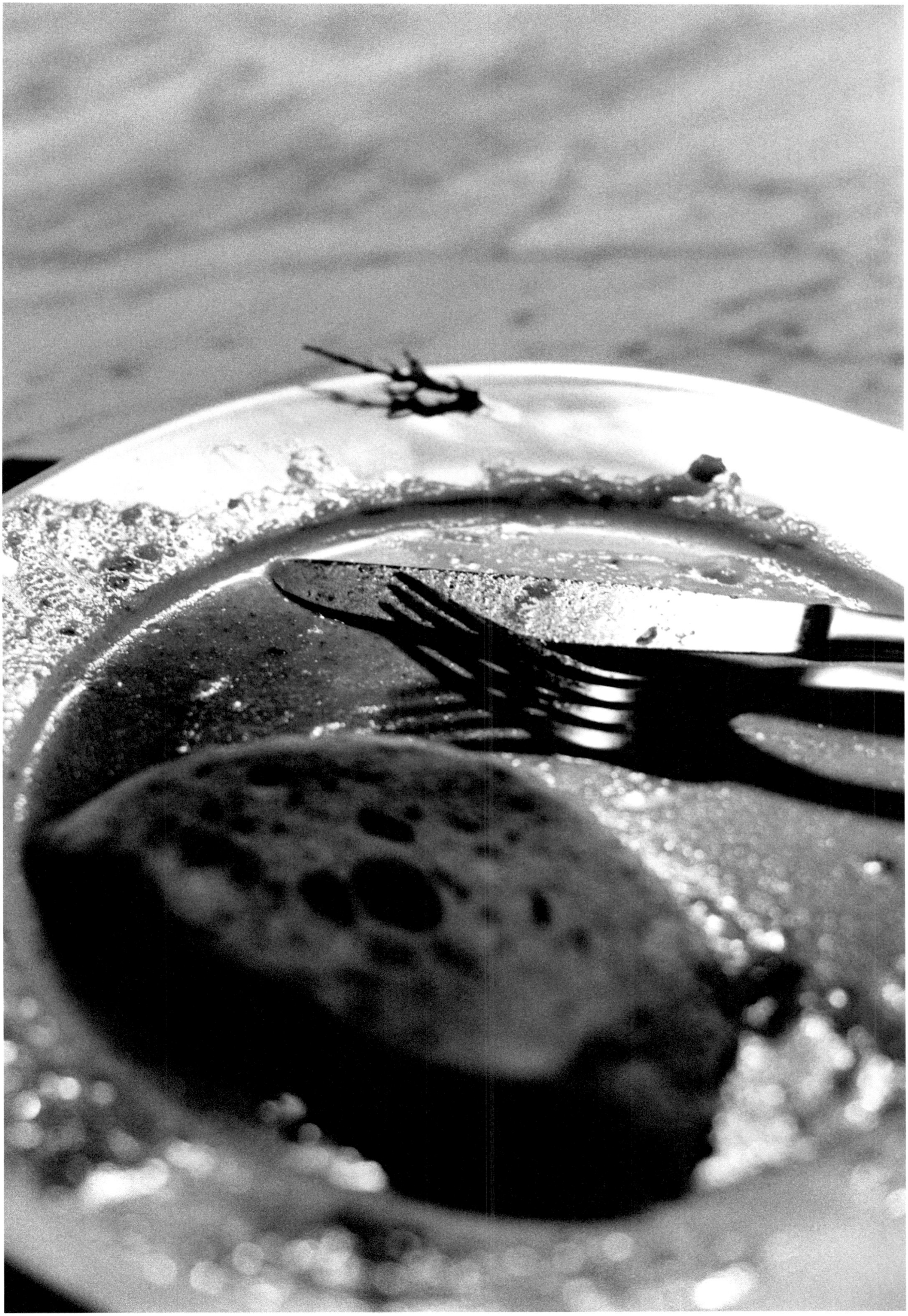

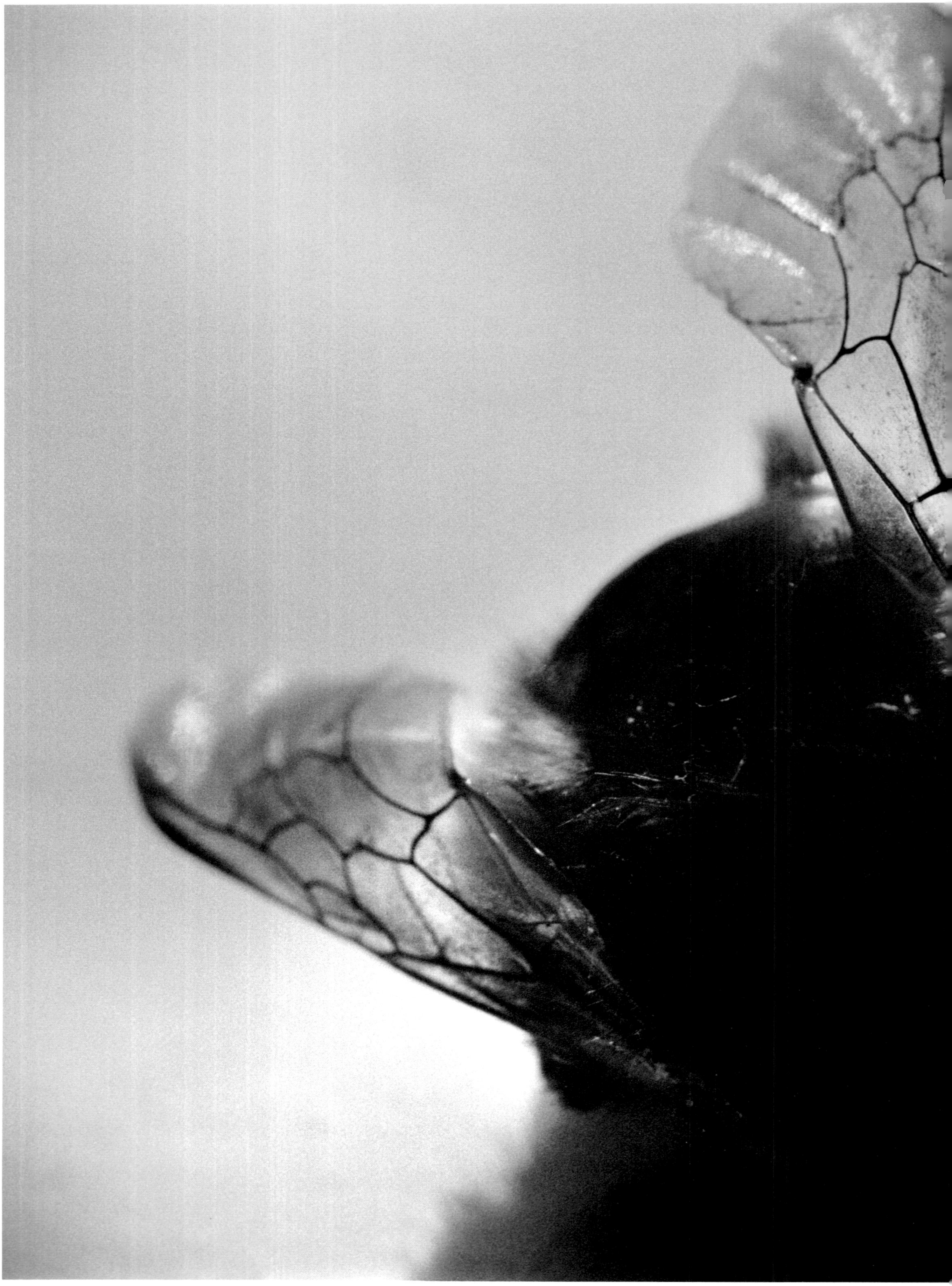

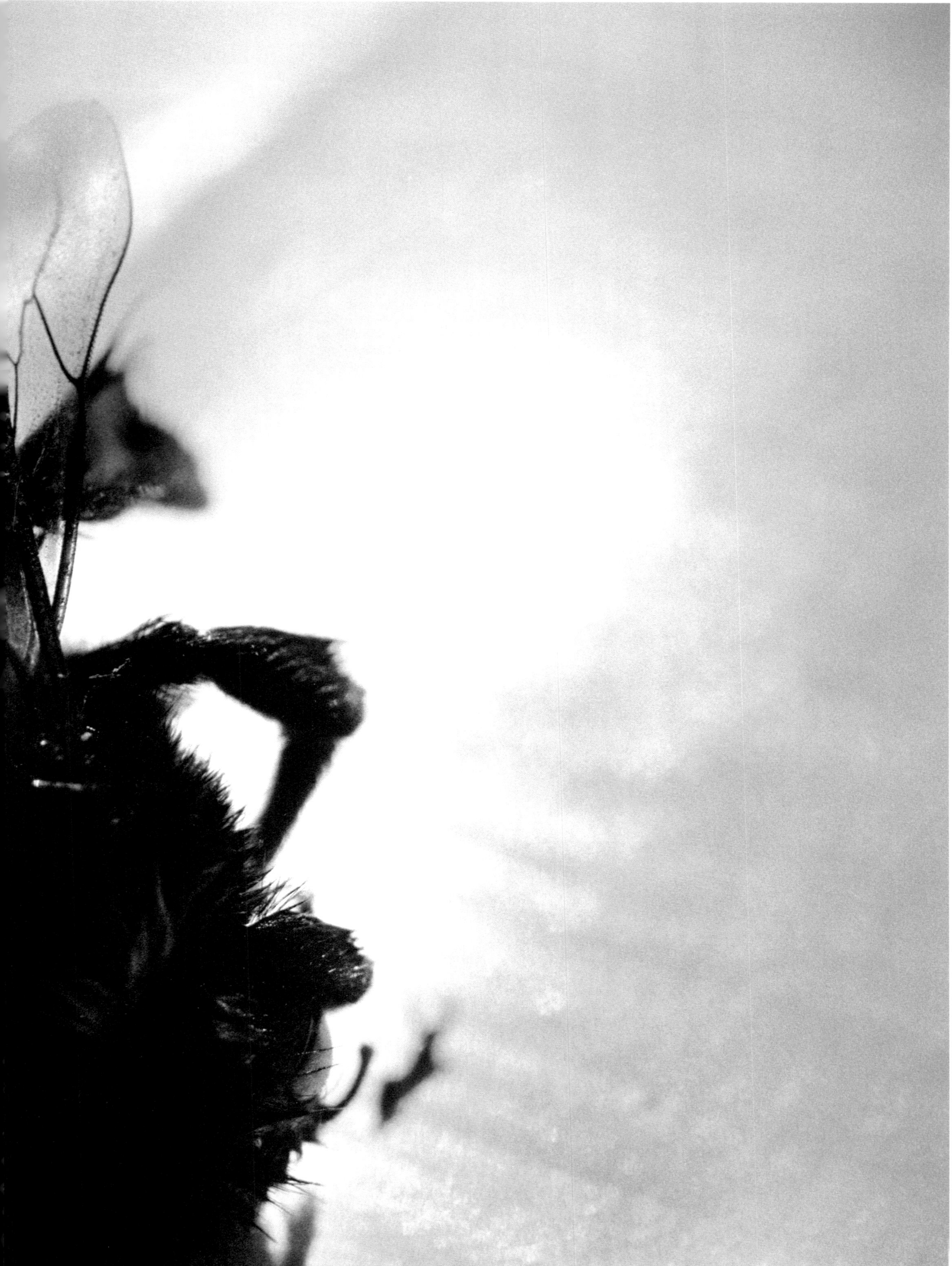

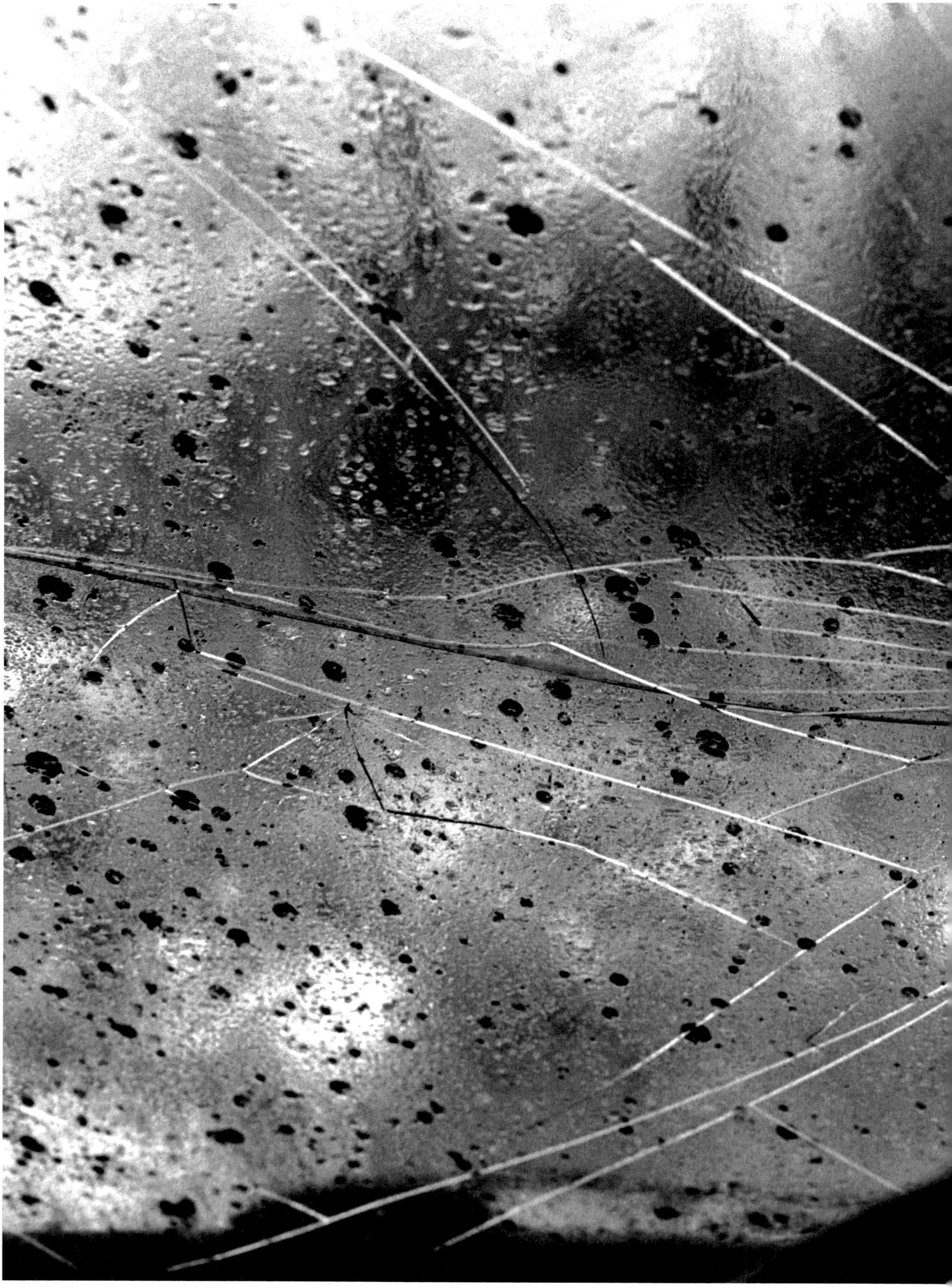

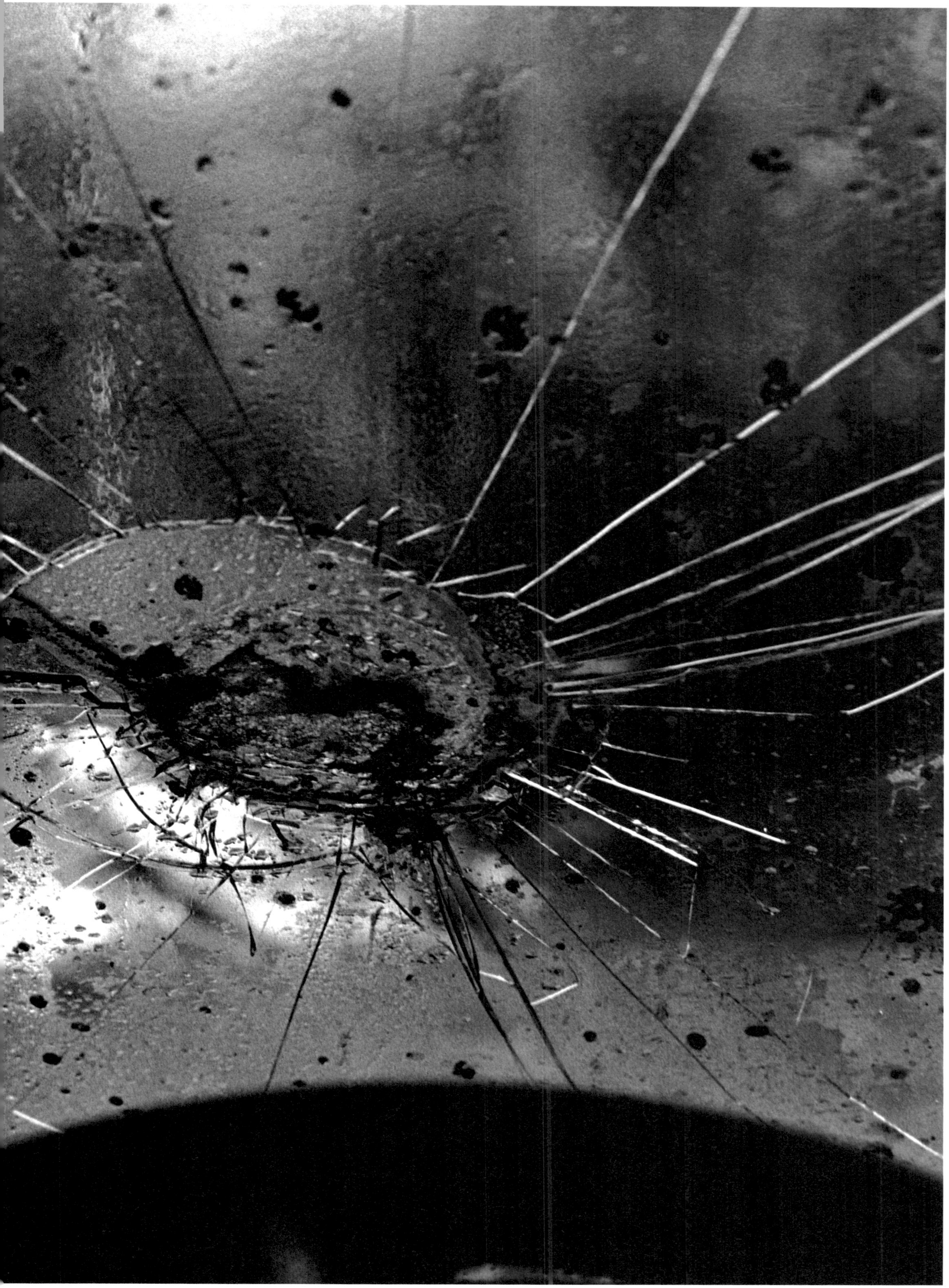

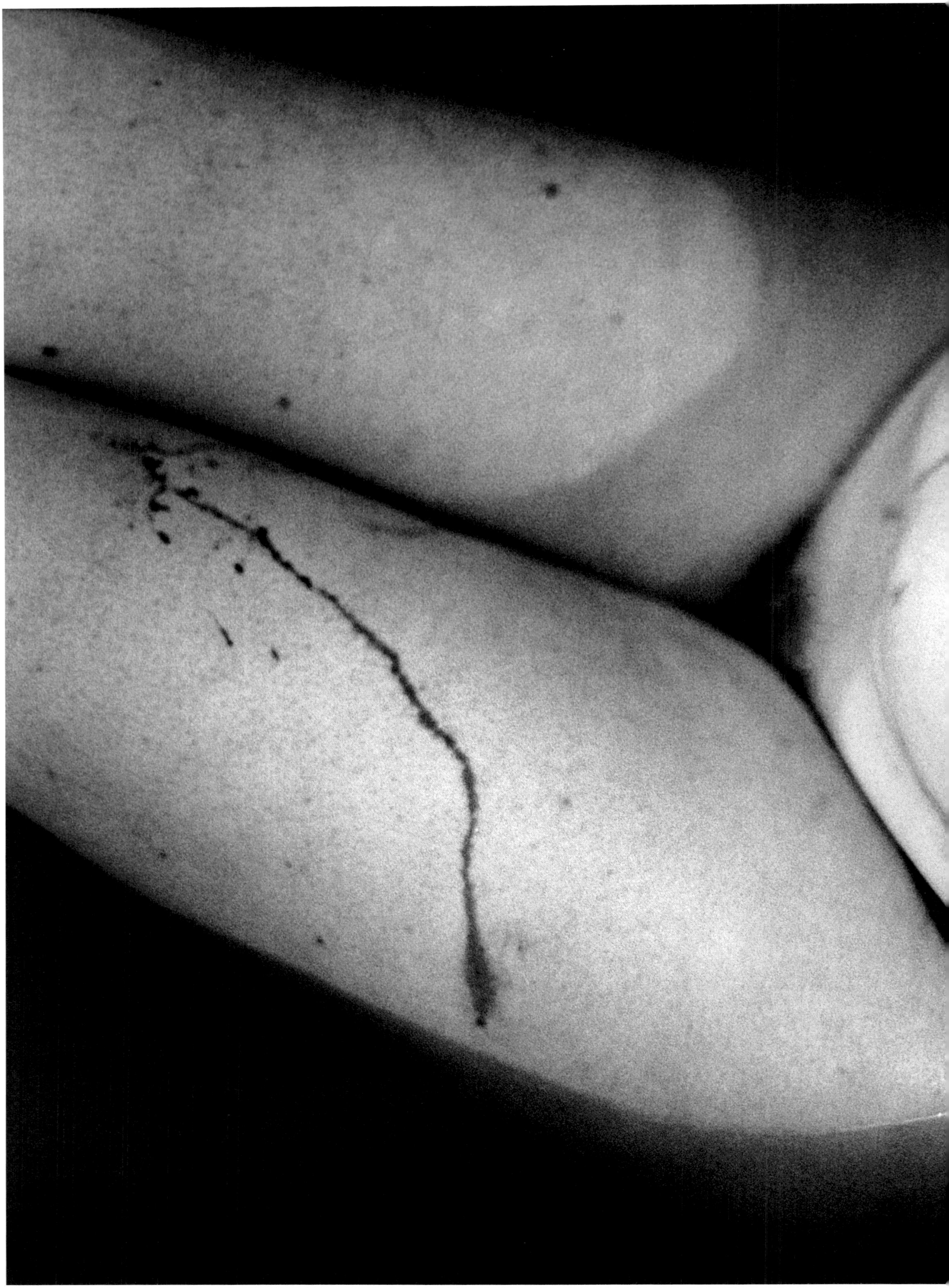

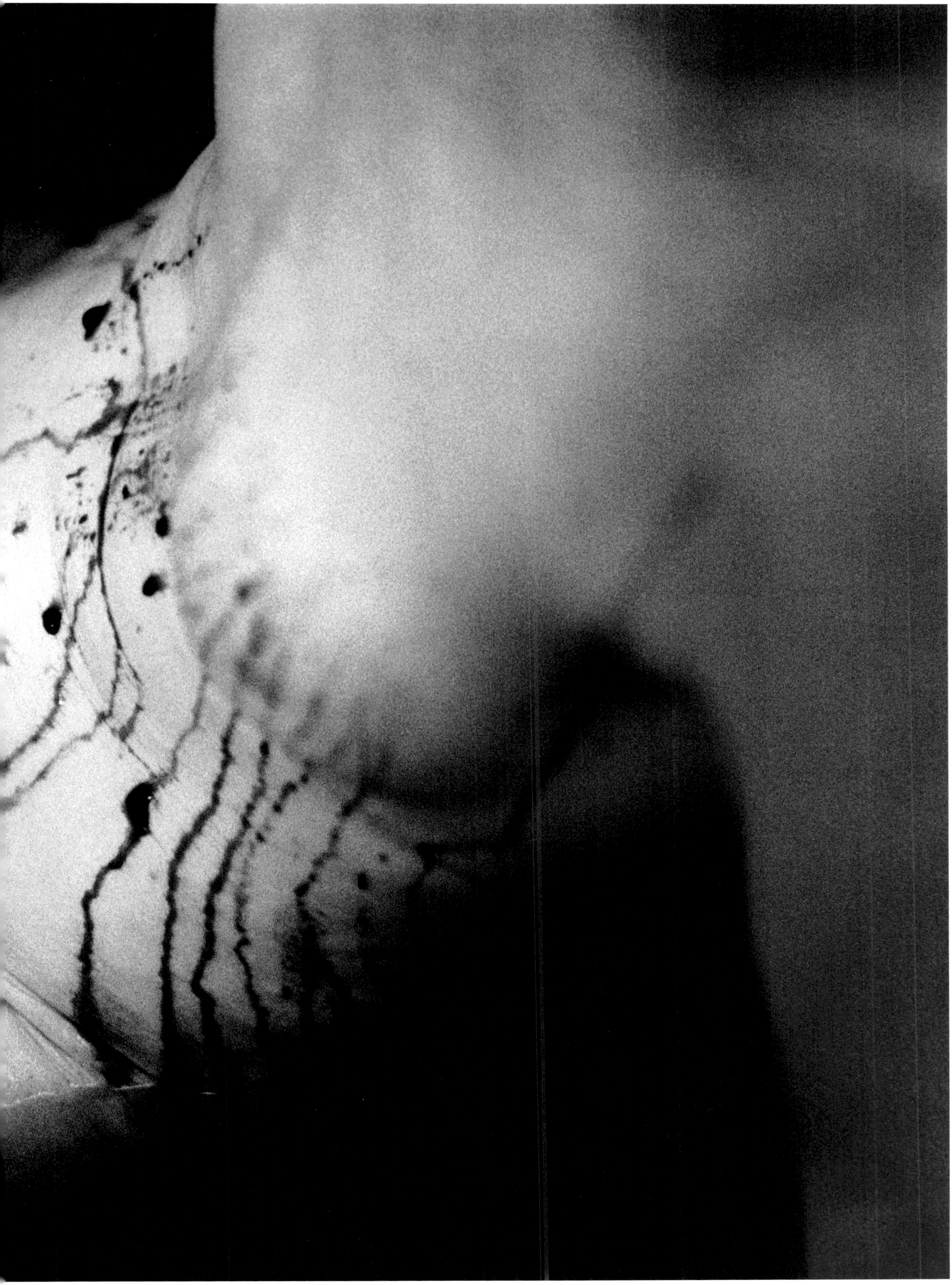

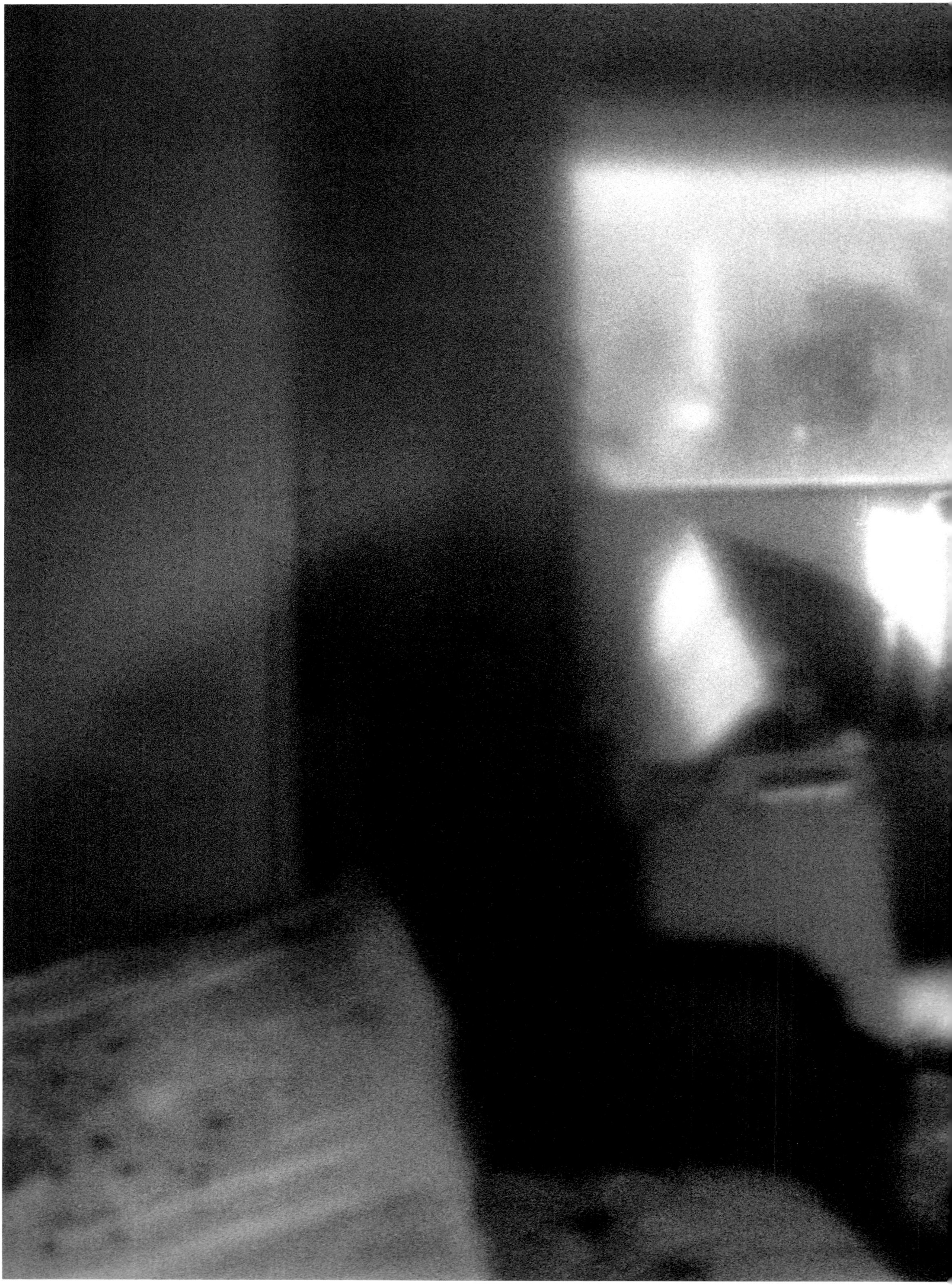

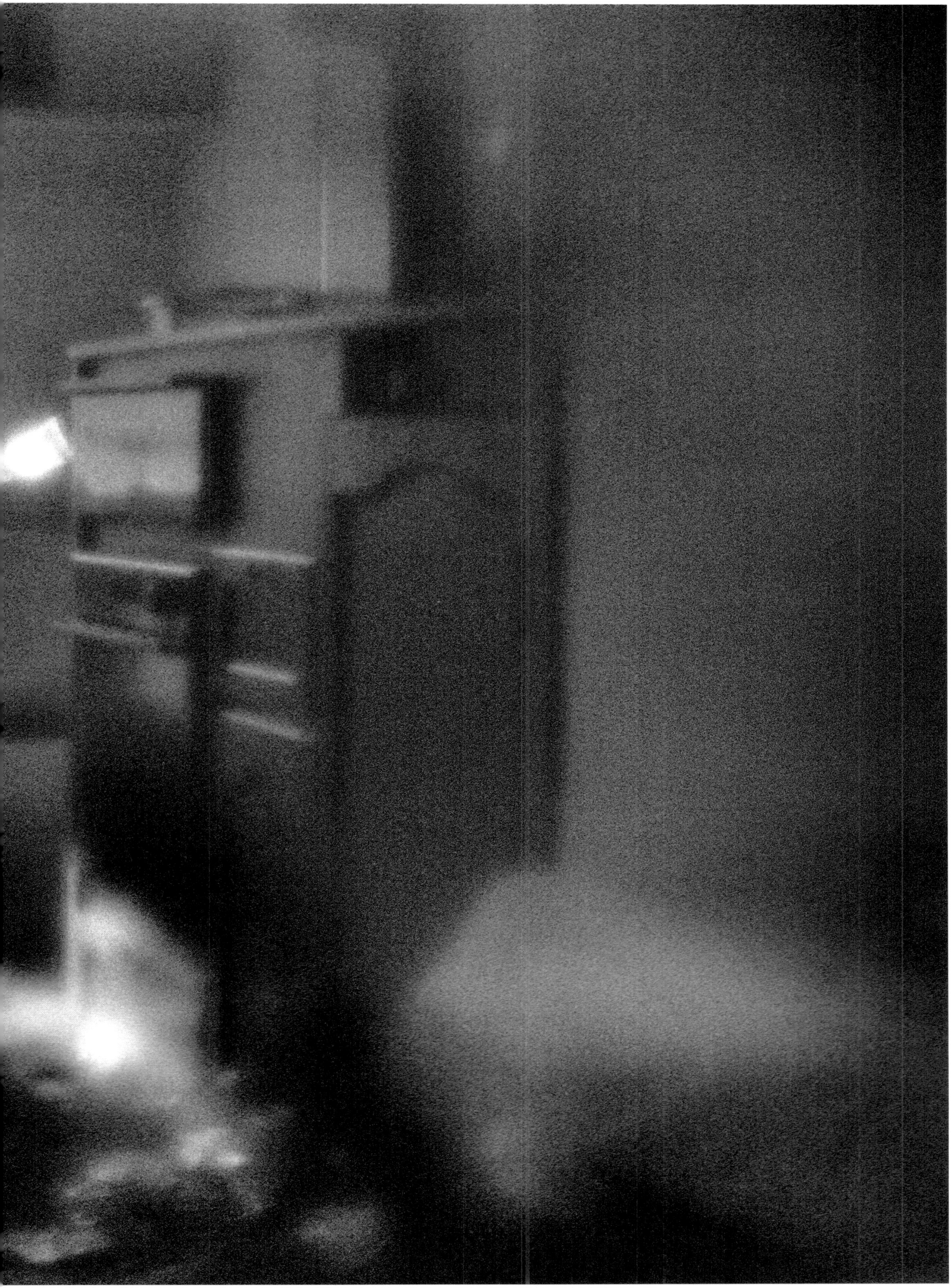

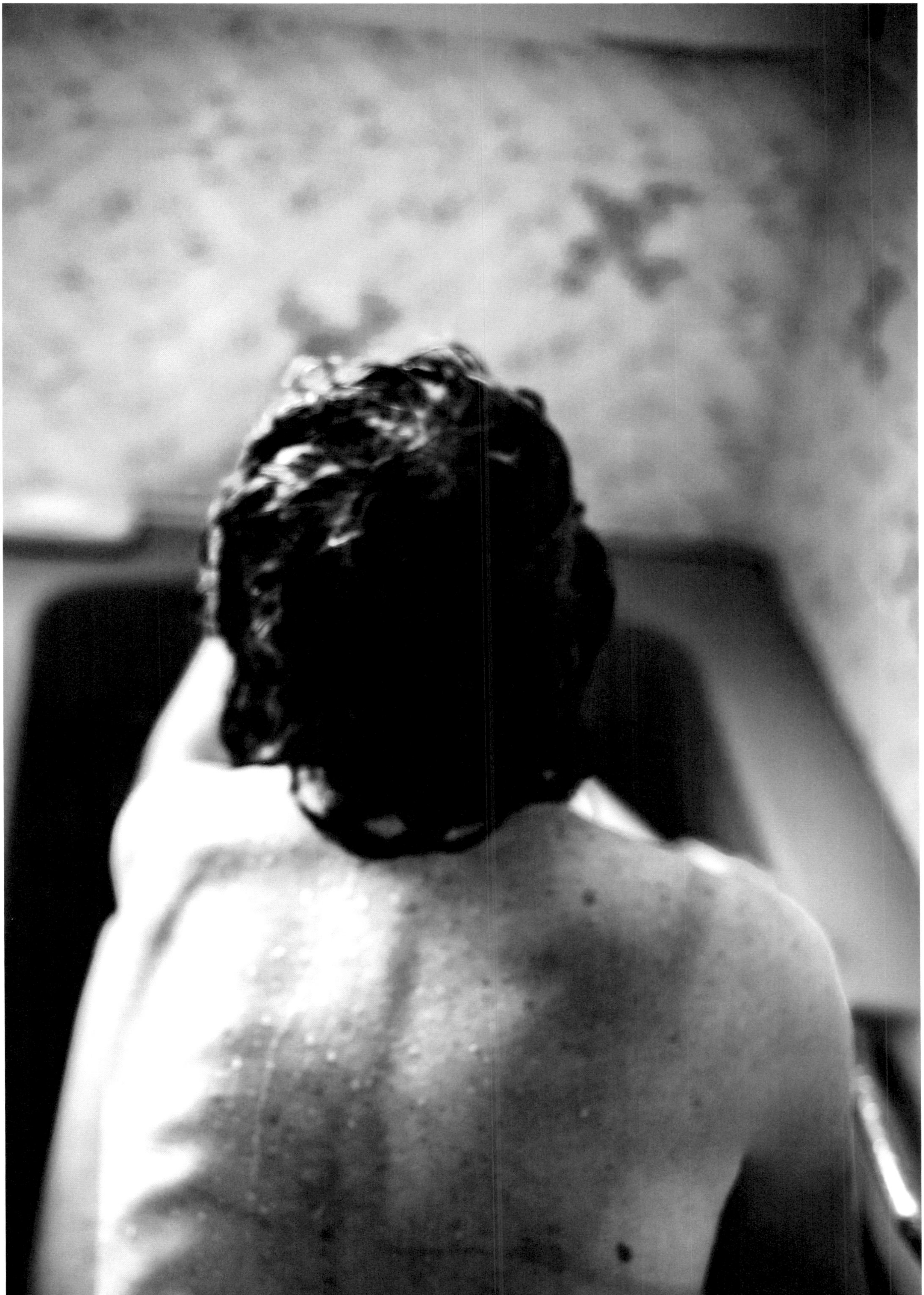

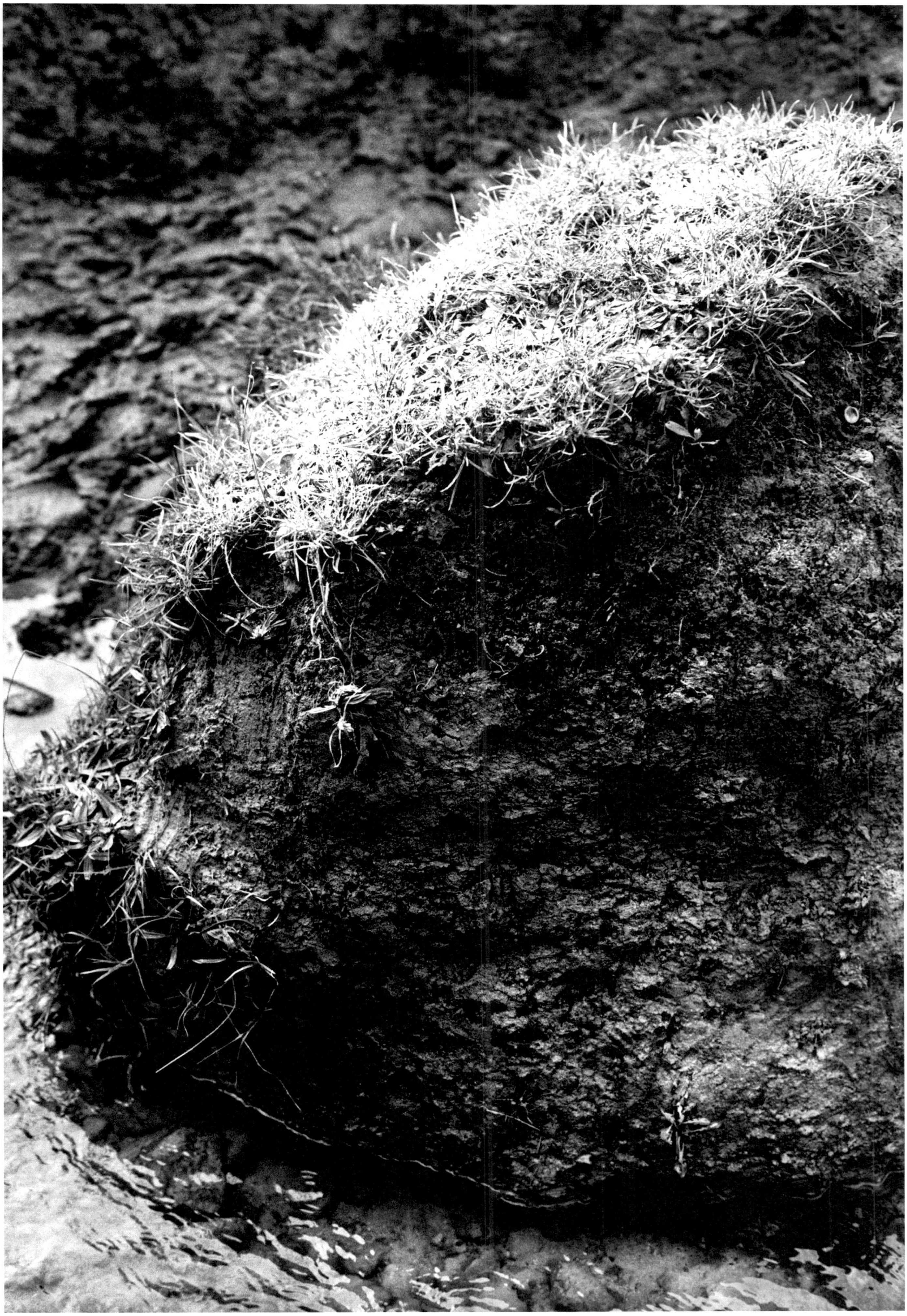

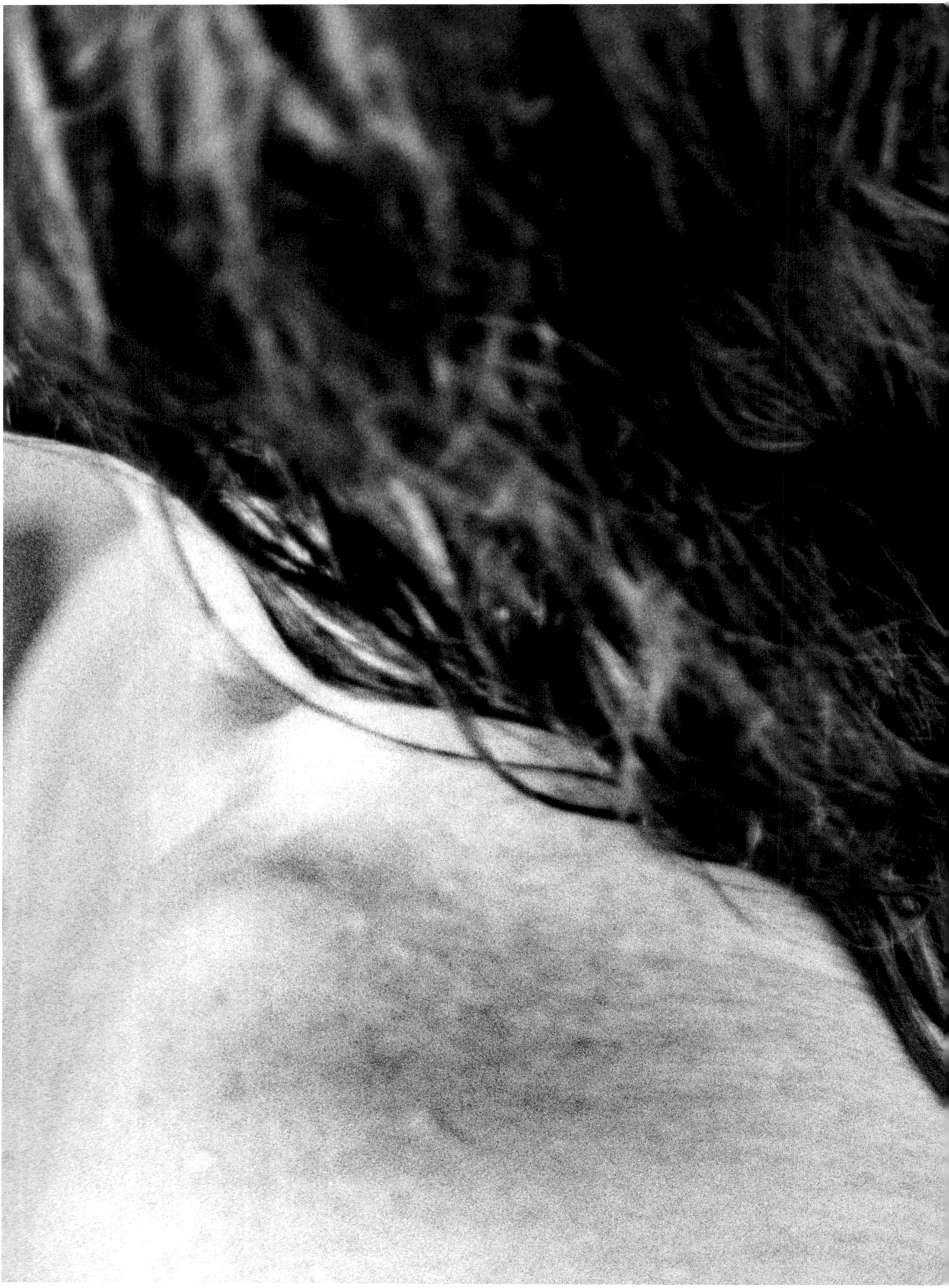

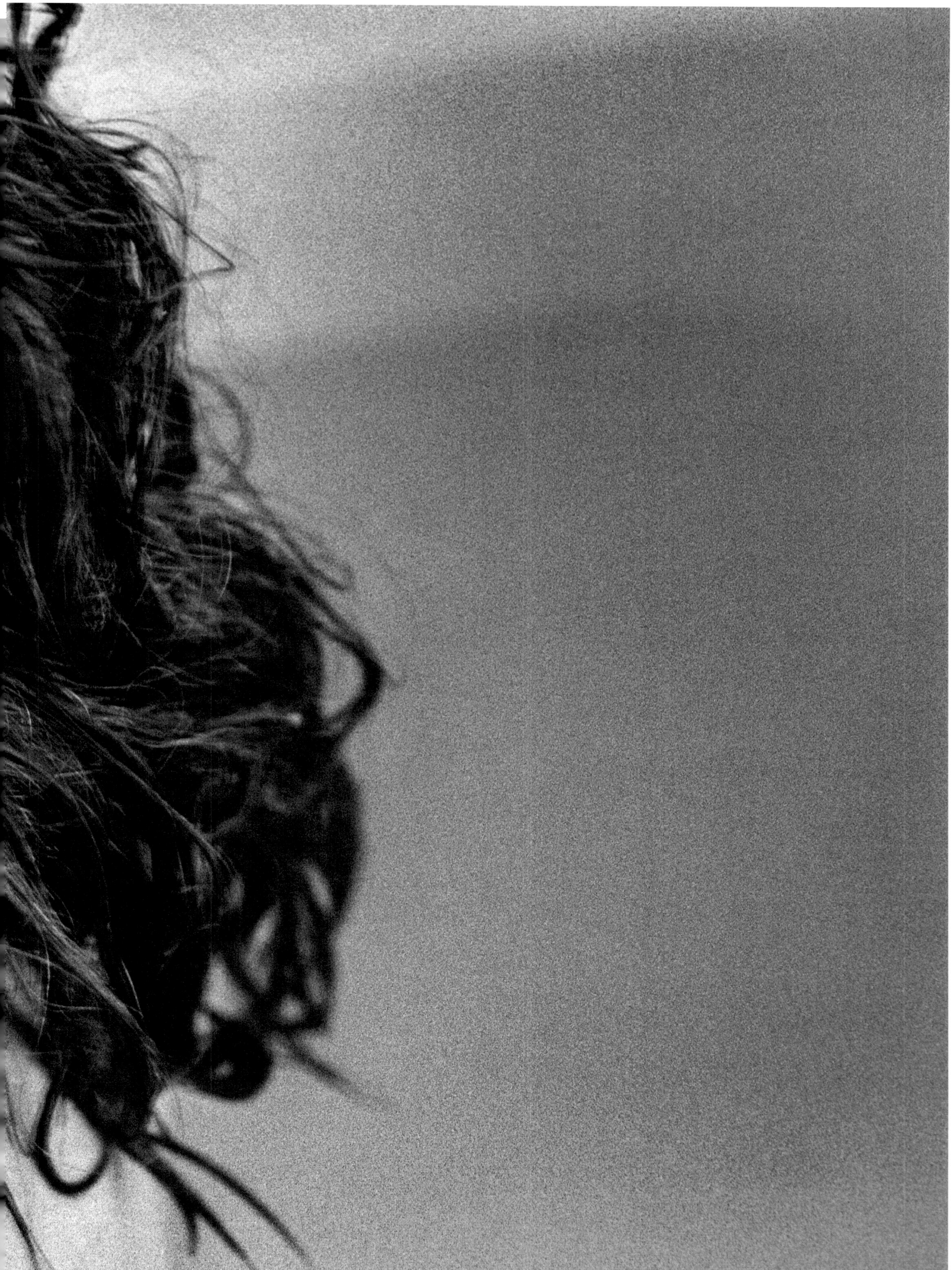

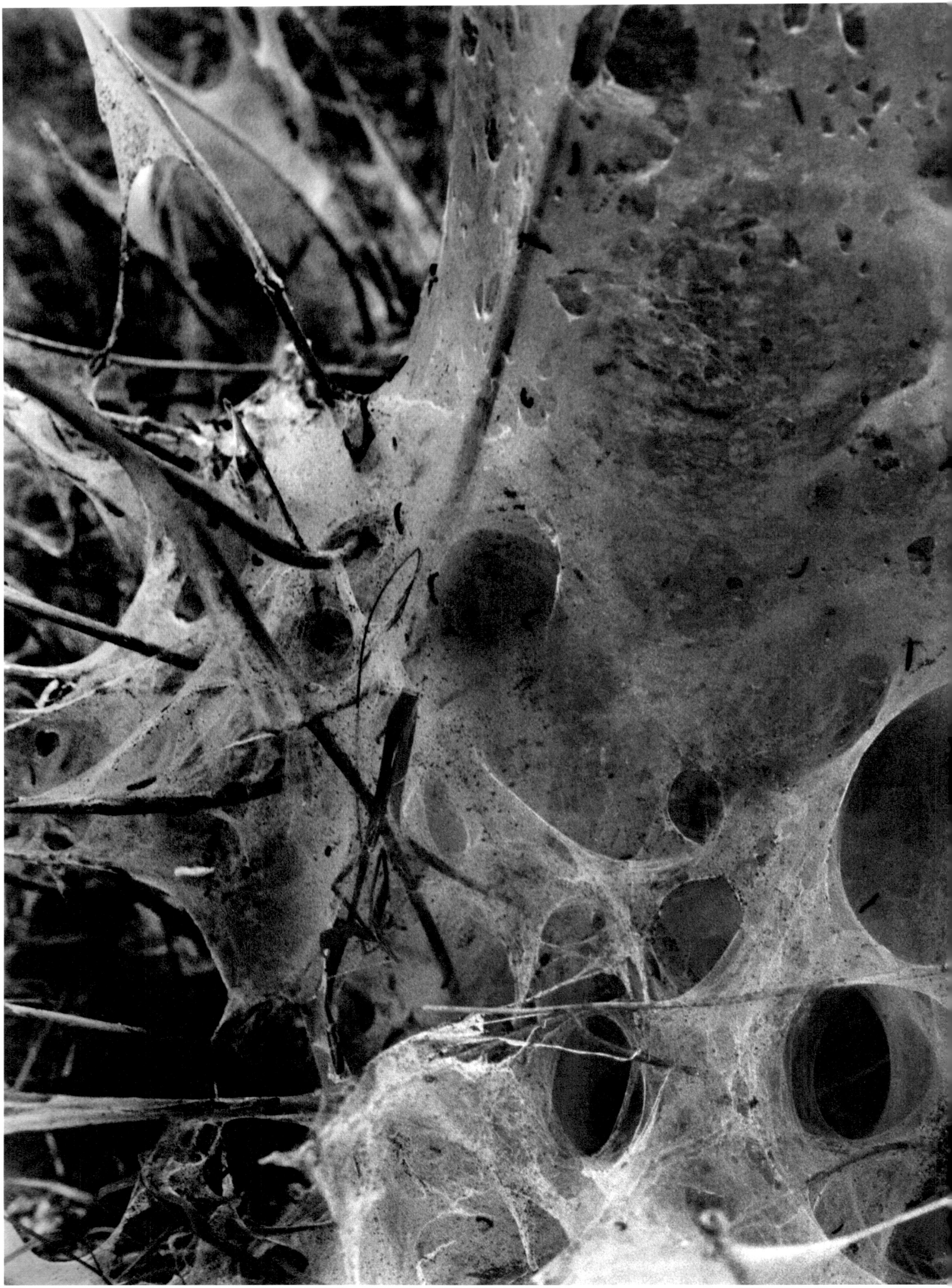

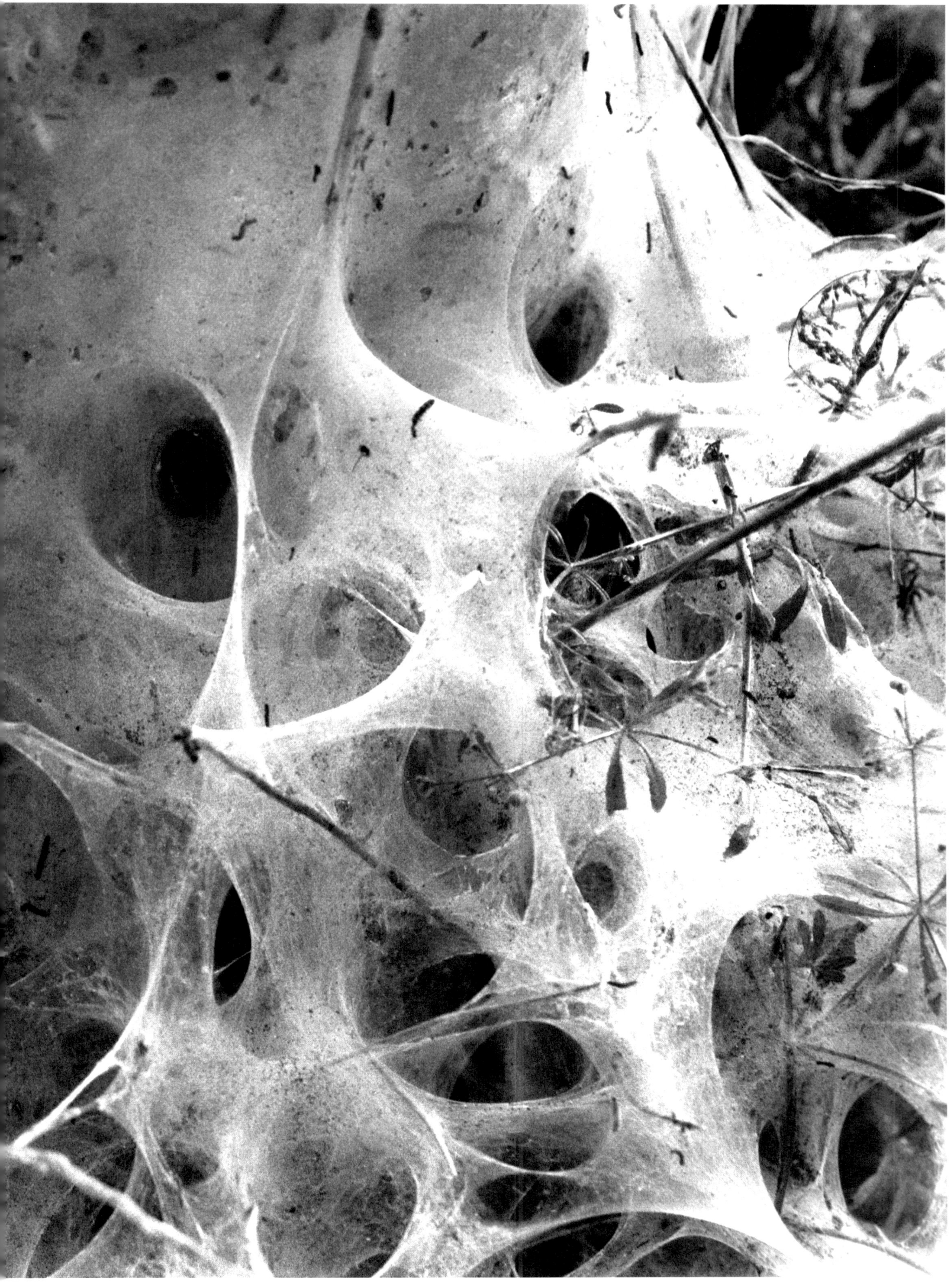

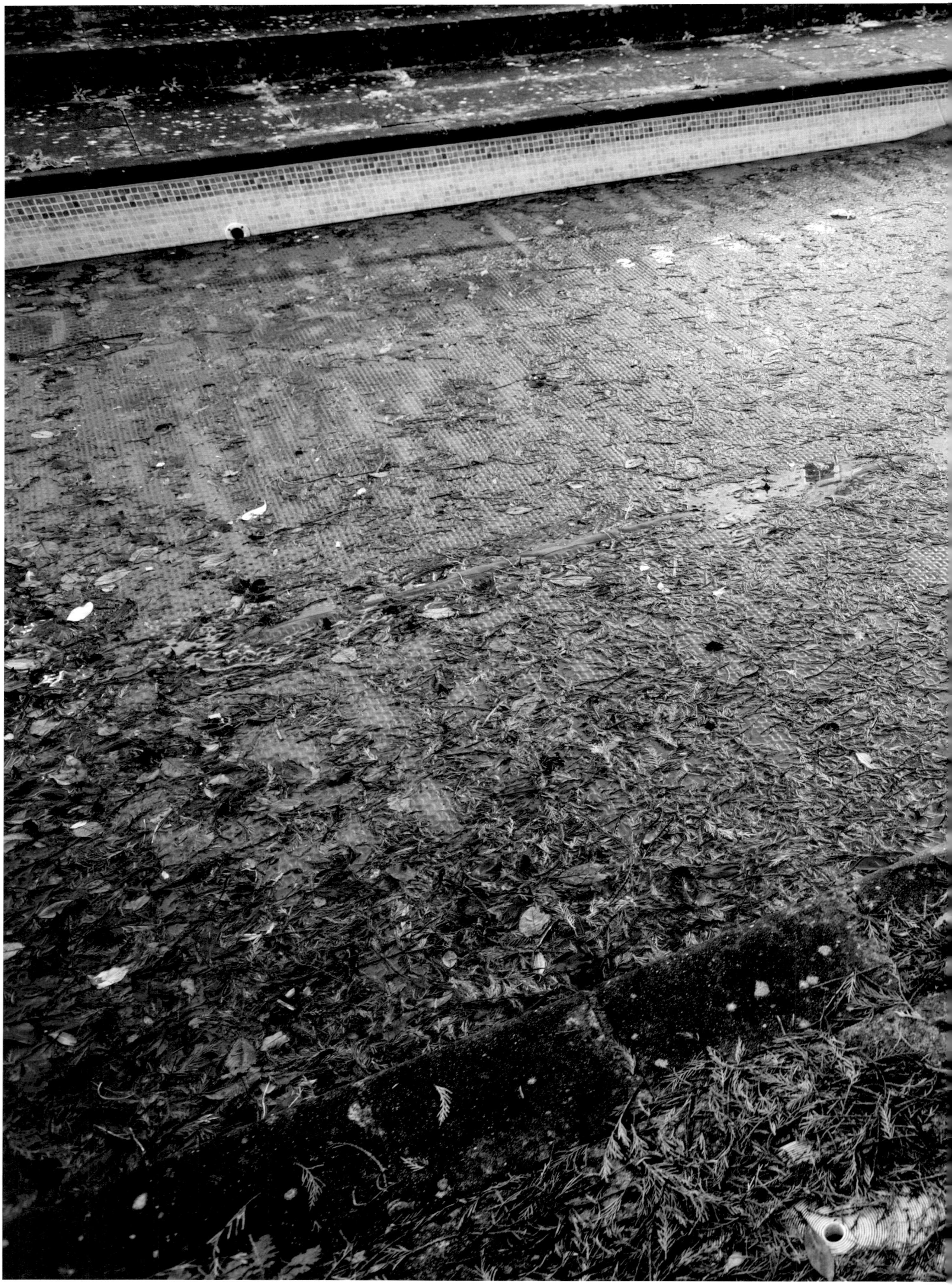

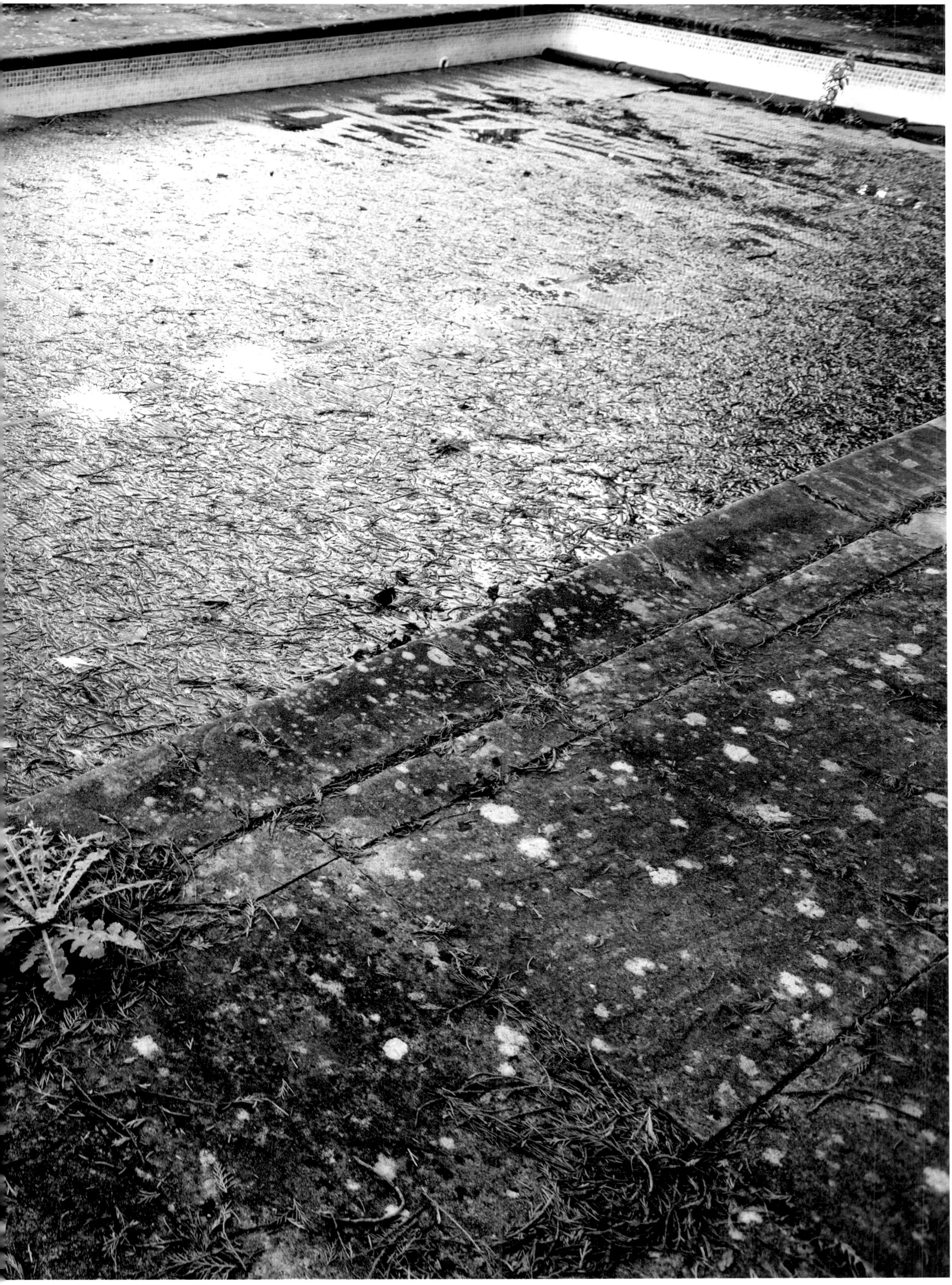

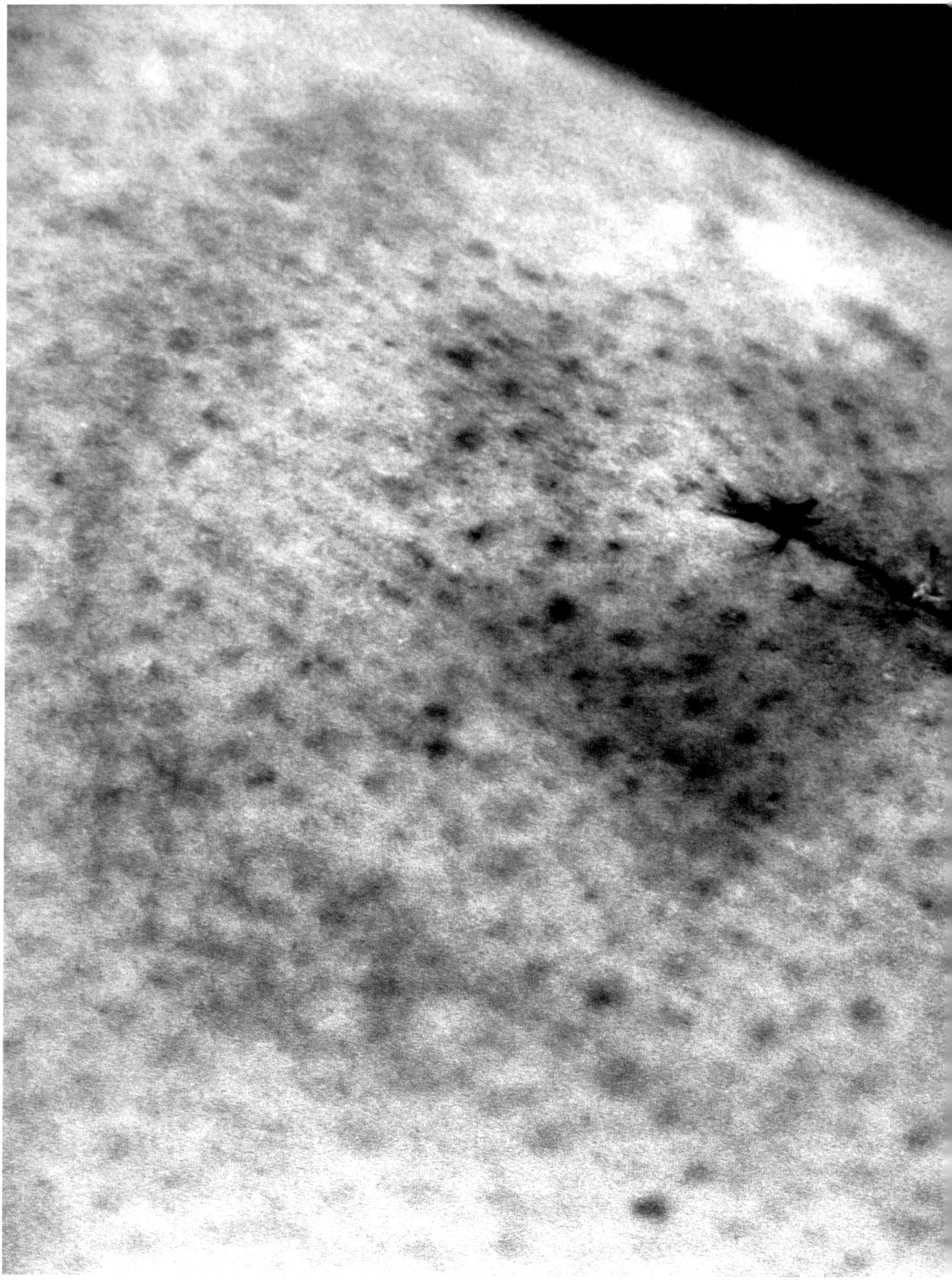

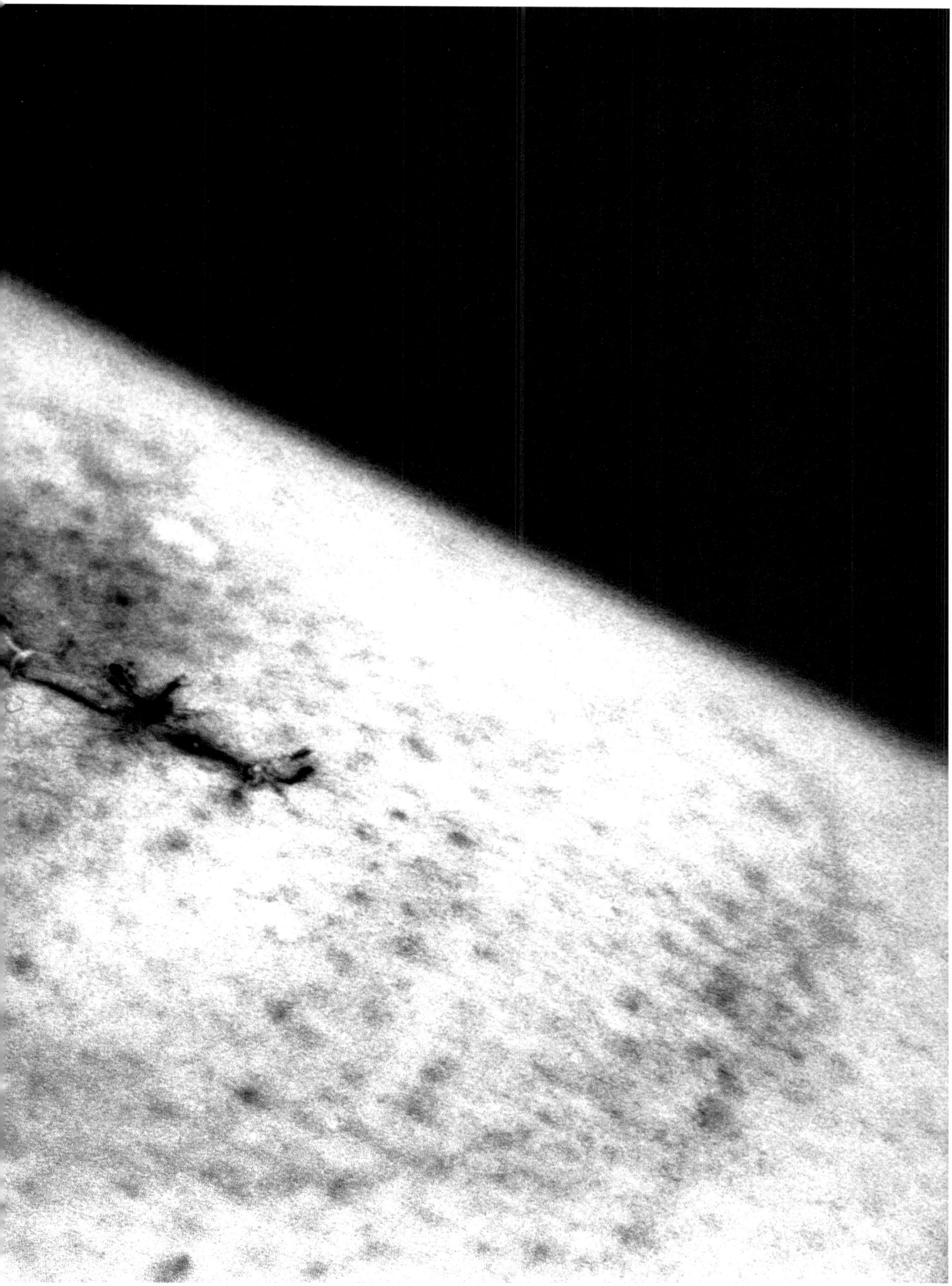

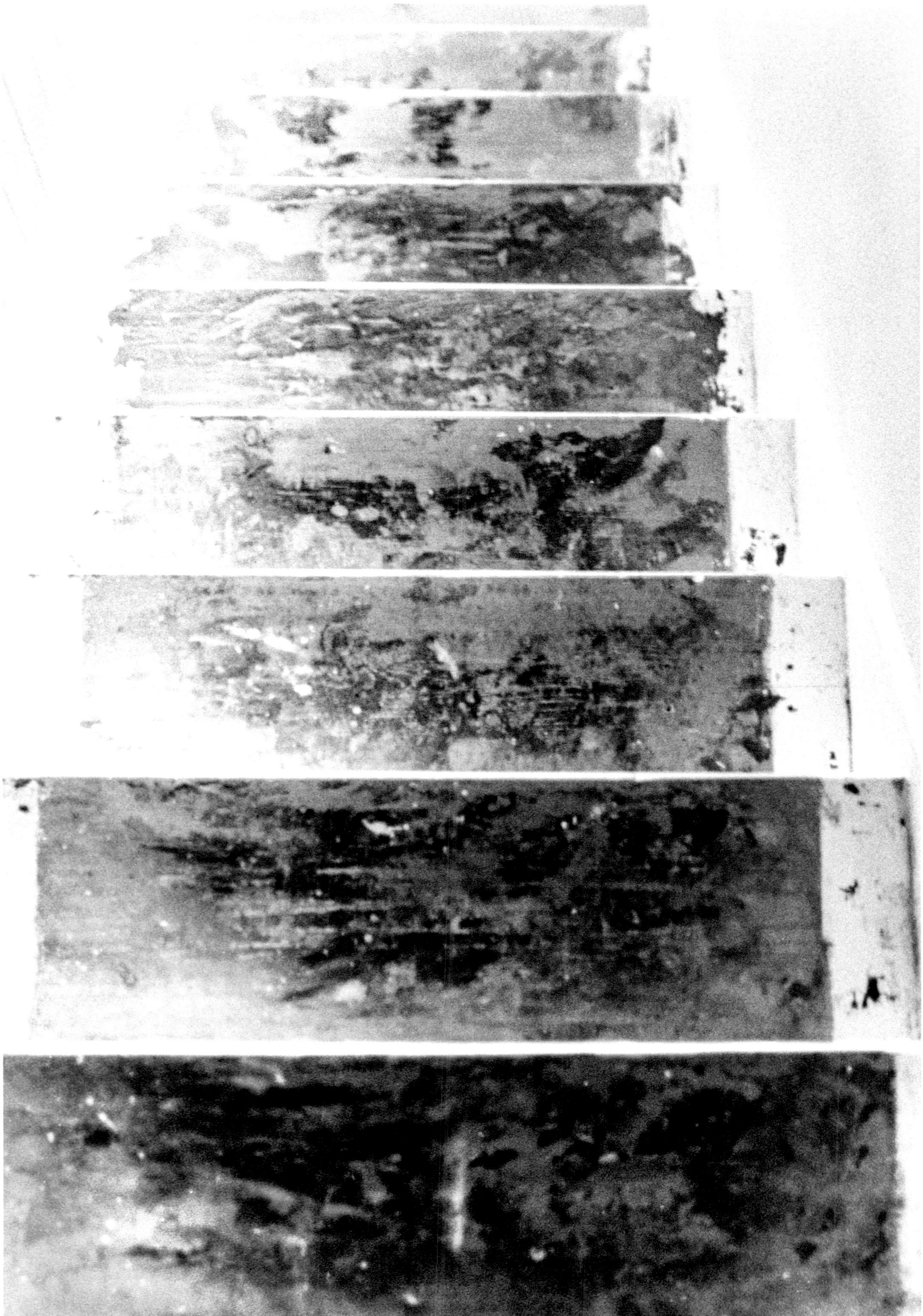

Communicated by: ProMED

Date: 30 Dec 2019
Communicated by: ProMed*

Wuhan unexplained pneumonia has been isolated test results will be announced [as soon as available]

On the evening of [30 Dec 2019], an 'urgent notice on the treatment of pneumonia of unknown cause' was issued, which was widely distributed on the Internet by the Medical Administration and Medical Administration of Wuhan Municipal Health Committee.

On the morning of [31 Dec 2019], China Business News reporter called the official hotline of Wuhan Municipal Health and Health Committee and learned that the content of the document is true.

Hotline staff said that what type of pneumonia of unknown cause appeared in Wuhan this time remains to be determined.

Another piece of emergency notification, entitled 'City Health and Health Commission's Report on Reporting the Treatment of Unknown Cause of Pneumonia' is also true. According to the urgent notice from a superior, the South China Seafood Market in our city has seen patients with pneumonia of unknown cause one after another.

The so-called unexplained pneumonia cases refer to the following 4 cases of pneumonia that cannot be diagnosed at the same time. After treatment with antibiotics for 3 to 5 days, the condition did not improve significantly.

It is understood that the 1st patient with unexplained pneumonia that appeared in Wuhan this time came from Wuhan South China Seafood Market.

Date: 31 Dec 2019
Patients with unknown cause of pneumonia in Wuhan have been isolated at multiple hospitals

Whether or not it is SARS has not yet been clarified, and citizens need not panic.

On [31 Dec 2019], an official report from Hubei Province said: 'Following the report of the Provincial Health and Health Commission, Wuhan has continued to monitor influenza and related diseases, and 27 cases of viral pneumonia have been found, all of which were diagnosed with viral pneumonia/ pulmonary infection Of the 27 cases, 7 were critically ill, and the remaining cases were controllable. The investigation found that most of the cases were operated from the South China Seafood City in Jianghan District, Wuhan. The National Health and Health Commission has decided to send an expert group to our province to guide the epidemic disposal on the morning of [31 Dec 2019]. At present, related virus typing, isolation treatment, public opinion control, and terminal disinfection are underway.'

On the evening of [30 Dec 2019], an 'Urgent Notice on Doing a Good Job in the Treatment of Unknown Cause of Pneumonia' issued by the Wuhan Municipal Health Commission circulated.

The document was verified by cross-examination. 'We are holding a special meeting on this,' said a medical worker at a famous 3rd-level hospital in Wuhan but it was clear that the cause to the patients was not clear. For more detailed information, it is temporarily inconvenient to disclose. At present, Wuhan Health and Health Commission official phone and official website are busy and unable to log in respectively.

Having been involved in moderating the SARS-CoV (severe acute respiratory syndrome - coronavirus) and the MERS-CoV (Middle Eastern Respiratory Syndrome - coronavirus), the type of social media activity that is now surrounding this event, is very reminiscent of the original 'rumours' that accompanied the SARS-CoV outbreak. The exception is the transparency of the local government in responding to this currently undiagnosed outbreak. While this report does not contain the tweets, there have been numerous tweets about this as yet undiagnosed outbreak.

Returning to the rumour mill, the discussion of this outbreak (a cluster of 4 or 7 cases) involves an 'atypical pneumonia.' and now additional information of apparently 27 cases, with 7 severe cases. More information on this outbreak including demographics of cases, possible known common contacts, and a clinical description of the illness would be greatly appreciated.

According to Wikipedia, Wuhan city is the capital city of Hubei province. It has an estimated population over 11 million inhabitants and is the largest city in central China, and the 7th largest city in all of China. Geographically it is in the eastern Jianghan Plain, on the Yangtze river's intersection with the Han River.

*Transcript sections from the first worldwide ProMed email alert from received and verified media sources regarding as yet unidentified Covid-19.
Sent to a global community of over 80,000 a few minutes before midnight on 31 December 2019.
Final notes and email by Dr Marjorie Pollack.

'International Society for Infectious Diseases Program for Monitoring Emerging Diseases'
ProMED With thanks

When I arrived at my parents' care home, my sister was already there, waiting in a silent building. The public spaces empty. Deserted reception desk.

We were taken to a room on the ground floor and asked to put on PPE: a gown, mask, and face shield. My memory tells me there were other items to put on as well, but I can't think what they could have been.

On the quiet second floor, we met with the floor manager who had known my parents and us for some years. We moved to an area optimistically called the music room. An oddly clipped and surreal conversation followed about my mum's condition. I can't recall much, but I do remember saying, 'So this is only going to go one way.' She nodded and said, 'Yes, possibly a day or two.' She added, 'I've lost nine this week already.'

Mum was under a cream interwoven blanket in her neat, tidy, well-presented room. She looked like a small, broken bird wrapped in a shroud. She recognised us or seemed to, which was not always the case and a bloody miracle considering we were in full PPE. No comprehension as to why, just an acceptance of the unknown.

Sarah and I sat on either side of her bed. What to say? Mum wanted some chocolate but could not chew or swallow it. She could not remember how to swallow water. In a voice much louder than normal, verging on fear, she asked, 'What shall we do? Help me.' Over and over. This is not what I had ever imagined, nor any of us. Conversation of sorts over the bed. Trying to remove chocolate from between her teeth and cheek. Dido comes to mind.

We sat for three, maybe four, hours. Illegal imposters in a silent building. A district nurse arrived to administer a morphine drip to her back. I held the hand of the smallest broken bird imaginable and said a goodbye I didn't believe, as it would never be sufficient.

In the corridor, Dad's door was ajar. He'd been asleep while we were with Mum. I saw his familiar silhouette against a window with partly drawn curtains, wearing a yellow jumper in his dimmed room. I hesitated, not wanting to disturb him, fearing confusion and distress. There would be time later, I told myself.

Every day since then, I have tried to convince myself I did that for his benefit rather than mine. My father died a few days after my mother. I said goodbye over the phone to a silent line.

For most of us, legacy is what we leave in our wake, the love and actions that define us, the strength we lend to others. Inevitably, guilt threads its way through this legacy, intertwined with everything else.

Will Green

For Michael and Jacqueline

This was going to start out as a different project—a body of work focusing on my home city of Bath from a perspective that others do not usually see.

Although the project was tentatively underway, with literally a few rolls of film processed in my bathroom, it quickly transmuted into a much more inward and emotional story as the effects of the Covid-19 pandemic started to rapidly take hold on the world and as for many, became a personal journey at home.

From early March 2020, I caught Covid-19 and lost both my parents to it within days of each other. This happened while I was suffering severely from and recovering from long Covid-19, which stayed with me into early 2021. *Death and Other Belongings*, is not so much a record of the external events, but rather a narrative study of the emotions and anxiety that came with the circumstances and the realisation of our fragility and mortality.

With thanks to:
Joanne Cope for always being my support and often reminding me to simply chop the wood and carry the water. To all the team at GOST Books: Rossella Castello, Katie Clifford, Gemma Gerhard, Justine Hucker, Allon Kaye, Eleanor Macnair, Claudia Paladini, Ana Rocha for their advice and help in leading me along the path of creating a book. Stuart Smith for seeing a book in a small and intimate story and for his vision and approach to creating the beautiful objects that are photobooks. And Mike Crawford for his advice and very last-minute end-of-week scans.

Death and Other Belongings
First published in 2024
by GOST Books, London

info@gostbooks.com
gostbooks.com

Edited and designed by GOST:
Rossella Castello, Katie Clifford, Gemma Gerhard, Justine Hucker, Allon Kaye, Eleanor Macnair, Claudia Paladini, Ana Rocha

Printed in Italy by EBS

British Library cataloguing-in-publication data.
A catalogue record of this book is available from the British Library.

ISBN 978-1-915423-59-7